———— THE NEW ILLUSTRATED GUIDE TO ————

MODERN
ATTACK
AIRCRAFT

SMITHMARK

MODERN
ATTACK
AIRCRAFT

MIKE SPICK & TIM RIPLEY

A Salamander Book

©Salamander Books Ltd. 1992

ISBN 0-8317-5054-5

This edition published in 1992 by
SMITHMARK Publishers, Inc., 112
Madison Avenue, New York, NY 10016.

SMITHMARK Books are available for
bulk purchase for sales promotion and
premium use. For details write or
telephone the Manager of Special
Sales, SMITHMARK Publishers, Inc.,
112 Madison Avenue, New York, NY
10016. (212) 532-6600.

All correspondence concerning the
content of this volume should be
addressed to Salamander Books Ltd.,
129-137 York Way, London N7 9LG,
United Kingdom.

This book may not be sold outside the
United States of America or Canada.

Contents

Credits

Authors: Mike Spick is the author of several works on modern combat aircraft and the tactics of air warfare, including Salamander's *Modern Air Combat* and *Modern Fighting Helicopters* (both with Bill Gunston).

Tim Ripley is a former research fellow at the University of Oxford. He now makes his living as a full-time author on modern military affairs.

Editor: Bob Munro

Designed by TIGA and Phil Gorton

Diagrams by TIGA

Filmset by The Old Mill

Color reproduction by Melbourne Graphics and Scantrans Pte.

Photographs: The publishers wish to thank all the official international governmental archives, weapons systems manufacturers and private collections who have supplied photographs for this book.

Printed in Hong Kong

Attack Aircraft

MODERN combat aircraft are extremely complex weapon systems which cost billions of dollars to develop. The almost uncontrollable escalation in combat aircraft prices has resulted in governments now demanding that they be able to perform a wide variety of roles, such as air superiority, strike, interdiction, close air support and anti-shipping. Jet engines, laser-guided bombs, radar-invisible "stealth" technology, computer targeting and in-flight refuelling have also made it possible for single- or two-seat aircraft to carry out long-range strategic missions that would previously have been the job four-engined heavy bombers. These trends make it extremely difficult to label modern military aircraft as pure "fighters" or "bombers".

The average dedicated attack aircraft has six or more hardpoints, each stressed for a different maximum loading and able to carry anything up to a dozen different stores whose weight and drag vary by a considerable amount and both of which affect performance. The mission profile is a factor also. High-altitude flight increases range: in the thin air drag is reduced and the engines burn less fuel, but this can realistically only be used in friendly or neutral areas; in operations over hostile territory low-level flight is the norm, and if afterburner is needed to maintain a high penetration speed, fuel is burned at an alarming rate which reduces range considerably. Range can be increased by carrying fuel externally in drop tanks, but this not only sterilises a hardpoint that might otherwise carry ordnance, thus reducing the weapons load, but tends to operate on a law of diminishing returns, something like half the fuel in the drop tank being used to carry the other half to the point where it materially affects the mission radius.

For the purpose of this volume we have taken the term "attack aircraft" to mean aircraft that are purpose-built to deliver bombs, missiles or gunfire on enemy frontline troops, supply lines or military targets deep in his home territory. Excluded are armed trainers, which have a limited air-to-ground capability and specialist air superiority machines, such as the F-15 Eagle or Su-27 Flanker. Large, multi-engined bombers, like the B-52 Stratofortress or Tu-26 Backfire, have also been left out because they are primarily designed to deliver nuclear weapons over long distances against strategic nuclear targets or cities.

Attack aircraft have to perform a wide range of missions. Strike missions are flown against strategic targets deep in the enemy's rear area, including hardened command posts, nuclear or chemical weapons facilities, communications sites, main naval bases, key industrial plants or oil refineries. Offensive counter-air missions are designed to destroy or prevent the enemy using his air

Below: The flat underbody of the Anglo-French Jaguar is well suited to ordnance carriage.

bases. Suppression of Enemy Air Defences missions are flown to ensure friendly aircraft are safe from enemy anti-aircraft (AA) artillery or surface-to-air missiles (SAMs). Attacks on supply dumps, supply convoys and key bridges on the enemy army's lines of communications are termed Air Interdiction, while attacks on enemy troops stationed behind the frontline in reserve positions are called Battlefield Interdiction. When aircraft are called in to attack the enemy army's frontline positions their operations are termed Close Air Support. Enemy shipping at sea is targeted by anti-surface warfare or maritime strike missions.

The actual performance of any modern military aircraft under any particular set of circumstances is something known only to the manufacturers and to the services that operate them, and what the manufacturers publish in their brochures are the best-case performance figures. These are of necessity rather bland and give little away. Vmax, for example, is usually stated for the aircraft in clean condition and at high altitude, regardless of the fact that it will rarely if ever be there in a war situation. By the same token, the ability to carry a mere two 500lb (227kg) bombs and deliver them on a target 500nm (925km) away tends to be of academic interest. More to the point is how far it can tote, say, 8,000lb (3,630kg) of bombs and still return to base with an acceptable fuel margin, taking into account that it may have to take evasive action at full throttle on the way in, and fight its way out after the attack.

Flight is a dynamic process and, external loads apart, the capabilities of an attack aircraft are constantly changing throughout the mission. Performance is modified by such factors as speed, altitude and ambient air temperature and pressure, while the weight of the aircraft lessens as fuel is burned. In a typical mission the aircraft would take off heavily laden and cruise-climb to altitude over friendly territory. Once there it would settle to an economical cruising speed, gradually burning off fuel and getting lighter until it approached enemy territory, when it would descend to low level to avoid radar detection and jettison empty fuel tanks to

reduce its overall drag factor.

Penetration of enemy territory would be made at high speed and low level, using fuel at a much higher rate. The weapons would then be deposited on the target, lightening the aircraft further and reducing drag, and the egress would be made at high speed and low level in what amounts to a clean condition. Once back in friendly airspace it would cruise-climb back to altitude and return to base at a fuel-burn optimised speed and height. Throughout the mission weight, drag and performance would have changed radically.

The data presented in the form of brochures and press releases is generally accurate for one set of circumstances. We have endeavoured to formulate a simple approach to aircraft data that will enable the reader to make valid comparisons between different types, without overstepping the constraints of security, by using the non-classified information that is freely available modified with common sense. In the case of Soviet aircraft it has been necessary to hazard an educated guess at some features, although guesswork has been kept to a minimum.

The format adopted for the tabular data and the reasons for its adoption are given where these are not self-evident. All data is given in both Imperial and Metric measures, in that order.

Length, wingspan and height are given in feet and metres. Wing area is given in square feet and square metres. Also stated is aspect ratio, which affects ride quality at low level.

Stated in pounds and kilograms, weights are often approximate and have sometimes been rounded off. Empty weight is generally the brochure figure where available, while clean take-off weight is the weight of the aircraft with full internal fuel and internal guns loaded. Maximum take-off weight is the brochure figure to which the aircraft has been cleared, often a paper figure based on the maximum weight that the hardpoints are stressed to carry, and in practice it is impossible to find a combination of weapons that matches each hardpoint exactly. Maximum external load is the sum total of the weights that the hardpoints are cleared to carry,

and the number of hardpoints is stated for air-to-ground stores: many attack aircraft have additional points for air-to-air missiles, ECM pods or fuel tanks.

The number and type of the engines are also stated. The thrust generated by one engine is stated in pounds and kilonewtons in terms of static thrust at sea level at both maximum (max) and military (mil) settings. In the dynamic conditions of flight these alter considerably, often giving more than the stated thrust at low altitudes but inevitably reducing as altitude increases, and it should be noted that turbofans (tf) are much more economical at cruise settings that the older turbojets (tj).

The quantity carried is stated in pounds and kilograms and for the purpose of standardisation, where volumetric figures only have been available, the weight of fuel has been calculated as being JP-4 at 6.5lb/US gallon. This may lead to marginal inaccuracies in places, but it does mean that like is being compared with like. Internal fuel is always given separately from external fuel. In-flight refuelling capability can be used to extend range to the point where the limiting factor becomes lubricant, oxygen or even pilot fatigue, but it is impractical when even remotely within range of enemy fighters.

Finally, the fuel fraction is the percentage of internal fuel expressed as a proportion of the clean take-off weight. Figures of 0.27 to 0.30 give aircraft with acceptably long-range performance on internal fuel; below 0.27 they tend to be lacking in operational radius, while above 0.30 they carry a weight penalty not only for the additional fuel, but for the weight of the tank and the structure needed to carry it. A turbofan aircraft should achieve a better radius of action for a given fuel fraction than one powered by a turbojet, although many other operational factors need to be taken into consideration.

Loadings are divided into two areas: thrust and wing. Thrust loadings are expressed as a ratio of static thrust to weight, giving a rough indication of available power comparisons between different types, although it is obvious that it will vary considerably between take-off with full fuel and full payload and the return to base with minimum fuel remaining and all ordnance expended. Thrust loadings are given for maximum take-off weight and for clean take-off weight, the spread between the two giving relative figures with which to compare different types.

Wing loading is stated in lb/ft² and kg/m² and is calculated over the same two loaded weights, clean take-off to maximum take-off. Wing loading is traditionally a measure of instantaneous manoeuvre capability for fighters, but high-lift devices have made the relationship more difficult to assess. In any case, a fully-laden attack aircraft will not be particularly manoeuvrable, but it will probably have to fly at high speeds at very low altitudes, where gust response is the most important factor.

Gust response is a measure of ride comfort; a low gust response prevents the crew being rattled about too much, a process that can degrade their efficiency considerably. As a general rule a high wing loading coupled with a low aspect ratio gives the lowest gust response and therefore the smoothest ride. The first figure, that for clean take-off weight, gives a rough idea of manoeuvre capability if the aircraft has to fight its way back to base.

Maximum speed, or Vmax, is given as Mach number, and is stated both for high altitude, normally 36,000ft (11,000m) and over, and for sea level. Such speeds are brochure figures for the clean condition, and as such are irrelevant for all but the homeward journey. As a general rule, all laden attack aircraft are firmly subsonic. The use of afterburner to gain speed simply offers a better target to heat-seeking missiles, consumes fuel more quickly and makes an accurate attack more difficult. When comparing the two figures for Vmax it should be borne in mind that the difference between the speed of sound at high altitude and at sea level is roughly 101.4mph (163km/h).

Service or operational ceiling is stated in feet and metres and being for the clean condition is also virtually irrelevant. Initial climb rate, given in ft/min and m/sec, is also a clean condition figure which is attained only at about Mach 0.9 at sea level. Take-off and landing distances are given in feet and metres. Other performance data is given in the text and is suitably qualified.

Below: A pair of RAF Tornados with a representative load of free-fall "dumb" bombs, fuel tanks and ECM pods.

Weapons Systems

ALMOST all modern attack aircraft continue to be fitted with automatic cannons of 20mm to 30mm calibre, or can carry cannon pods. This is partly to provide a last line of defence against marauding enemy fighters, but it is also to deal with certain types of ground targets and allow for the failure of more sophisticated weapon systems. The classic use of aircraft cannon armament is to strafe enemy forces, particularly convoys of soft-skinned vehicles. Except against very exposed targets this is not now a common tactic because the attacking pilot has to fly his aircraft straight and level to lay its gun on target — not a very healthy thing to do when faced with modern air defence weapons. Western aircraft are generally equipped with rotary/gatling gun weapons, such as the 20mm M61A1 Vulcan on the F-16 Fighting Falcon or the 25mm GAU-12/U Equaliser on the AV-8B Harrier II. The latter has a rate of fire in excess of 3,600 rounds per minute at a range of approximately 3,281ft (1,000m).

The A-10A Thunderbolt II tank-busting aircraft is unique in that it is purposely designed around the 30mm GAU-30 Avenger cannon. To enable pilots to fly close enough to enemy positions to acquire targets and survive anti-aircraft fire directed at them, the A-10A is heavily armoured and incorporates other design features so it can take multiple hits and still get back to base. Pilots who attacked Iraqi tanks during the Gulf War were able to hit stationary targets at up to two miles (3.2km) range and the GAU-30's depleted uranium shells penetrated every type of tank in Iraqi service including the Soviet-made T-72.

Bombs are the traditional weapon of attack aircraft. Their design, however, has advanced considerably since the end of the Second World War. Old-fashioned high-explosive (HE) "dumb" bombs are still used in large numbers, but there are now specialist types available, including cluster bombs with sub-munitions for hitting "area" targets such as infantry positions, penetrator bombs to destroy hardened bunkers and laser-

Right: Though its ability to lay down a carpet of bombs is highly impressive, the B-52 is a bomber, not an attack aircraft.

Below: At the other end of the scale, the SOCATA Guerrier is too lightly armed to qualify as a genuine attack aircraft.

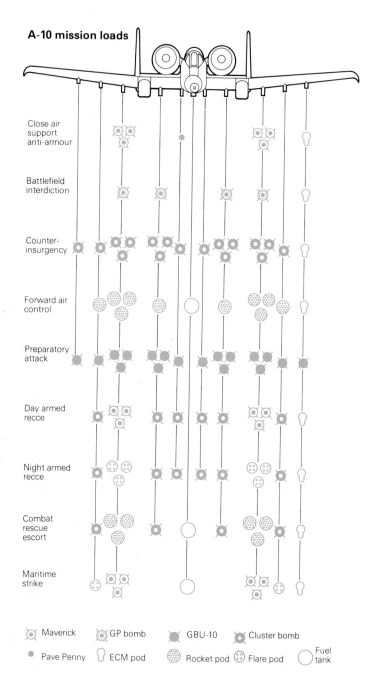

A-10 mission loads

Close air support anti-armour

Battlefield interdiction

Counter-insurgency

Forward air control

Preparatory attack

Day armed recce

Night armed recce

Combat rescue escort

Maritime strike

Maverick　　GP bomb　　GBU-10　　Cluster bomb

Pave Penny　　ECM pod　　Rocket pod　　Flare pod　　Fuel tank

Above: The types of weapons to be carried by today's attack aircraft (an A-10A and a full range of ordnance being shown) are primarily determined by the nature of the mission and its operational objectives. In reality, however, problems of a logistical nature can often restrict the availability of specific ordnance; a fact of life during the Gulf War.

guided "smart" bombs for pin-point impact accuracy.

Typical of modern bombs are the US general-purpose Mk.82 500lb (227kg), Mk.83 1,000lb (454kg) and Mk.84 2,000lb (907kg), which are also in service with many other air forces. They come with standard HE warheads, which can be fitted with various modifications to improve performance in different attack scenarios. American pilots who used the bombs in the Gulf War reported that the blast from their HE warheads was devastating if a direct hit was scored on tanks, other armoured vehicles, dug-in artillery pieces or buildings. A near miss from a Mk.84 bomb was also reported to be reasonably sure of knocking out an armoured vehicle.

To help pilots get their bombs on-target, most attack aircraft now feature computerised navigation/attack systems, such as the Hughes angle/rate bombing system fitted to the AV-8B, or the new low-altitude safety targetting enhancement system on the A-10A. These systems calculate the effect of wind, aircraft speed, air pressure, g-loading, bank angle, altitude, rate of descent and other factors on the ballistic trajectory of bombs. All these factors can affect whether bombs will hit or miss and to what degree. Different attack profiles create their own problems. At low level strong air turbulence can

Above: The maximum load of air-to-ground weapons carried by a single F-111 is amazing, though a combat load would be much less. The groupings show the total load for each type. No "smart" or stand-off weapons are shown—the F-111 was supposed to make them unnecessary.

affect accuracy and can also result in bombs not having enough time to arm themselves properly, as was the case with Argentine bombs during the Falklands War. Retard mechanism such as that used on the American Snakeye system are meant to solve this problem.

Computers have taken much of the guesswork out of bomb aiming and tremendous strides have been made in bombing accuracy. The Israeli raid on the Iraqi Osirak nuclear reactor in June 1981 showed that bombs could be delivered accurately into a very small target area, while US pilots scored a number of hits on Iraqi tanks with Mk.82, Mk.83 and Mk.84 bombs in the Gulf War. Such accuracy, however, is far from the norm and very benign conditions are needed to make bombs go exactly where they are intended. Once a bomb leaves its carrying aircraft its flight path is far from predictable. Unstable ballistics and unpredictable, erratic winds can force bombs off target by a wide margin. At low altitudes this is not so

Left: Though unable to carry out the full range of their attack mission options during the Gulf War (due, in part, to the lack of LANTIRN targeting pods in-theatre), USAF F-16s still played a major role in the air campaign. Note The Rockeye II unguided free-fall cluster bomb beneath the port wing.

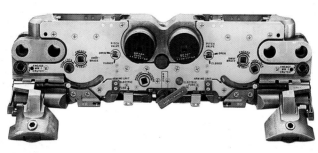

much of a problem, but when attack aircraft are operating from medium or high altitudes the margin of error obviously becomes considerably greater. Circular Error Probable is the technical term for the likely margin of error. Things can be made even worse if the pilot is trying to manoeuvre his aircraft to avoid enemy anti-aircraft (AA) fire or surface-to-air missiles (SAM). This was the case during Operation *Desert Storm*, where US aircraft were ordered to operate at over 12,000ft (3,657m) to stay out of Iraqi AA range. On many missions high-flying F-16s or F/A-18 Hornets proved unable to hit point targets such as specific buildings or runways even with the aid of their sophisticated targeting computers. USAF F-111Es on high altitude bomb runs usually got their

bombs within 40ft (12.19m) of the target compared to under 6ft (1.82m) during the extremely low-level attacks on the opening night of the war.

One solution to this age-old problem is to use what are called cluster bombs. They scatter smaller sub-munitions or bomblets out to devastate a large area and are intended for use against small or dispersed targets such as infantry positions, tank formations, artillery and soft-skinned vehicle convoys. US airmen who bombed Iraq called this the "shotgun" school of bombing. Cluster bombs such as the British BL.755, American CBU-52/59 Rockeye II series or the more modern CBU-87/89 CEM series, are dropped from aircraft and at pre-set altitudes, break open and start scattering hundreds of sub-munitions over the target area. These can be anti-personnel weapons which then explode and fill the air above a wide area with deadly red-hot shrapnel. Anti-tank sub-munitions are fitted with whole-charge warheads to penetrate tanks' weak top armour.

A percentage of the sub-munitions are also fitted with delayed-action fuses to make the target area dangerous for anyone who survives the initial attack.

Cluster bombs were used on a large scale for the first time in the Gulf War to devastating effect. The scale of their use can be gauged from the

Above left: BL755 cluster-bombs tumble on leaving a CF-18A Hornet. The clean release of stores is alway a problem

Left: Ejector release units like this EDO Model 805 are needed to ensure the safe separation of munitions

Below: Close support weapons such as these BAT 120 bombs need special adaptors for rapid sequential release.

Release

Retardation

total figure of 26,000 Rockeye IIs used by US forces in the conflict. Iraqi infantry who were on the receiving end of cluster bomb sub-munitions called them "black rain". There were many unusual uses of cluster bombs. For example, USAF Wild Weasel units found them very effective for destroying SAM and radar sites, which were very vulnerable because of their delicate antennae and other electronics. US Naval aviators also found them very useful against lightly-protected Iraqi patrol boats and sprawling naval bases. Post-war analysis suggests that some 20 per cent of US sub-munitions did not detonate as intended, leaving the Kuwaiti desert littered with deadly unexploded ordnance.

Some US cluster bombs can dispense Gator anti-armour mines that enable instant minefields to be created in the path of enemy mobile units. When Iraqi troops tried to escape from Kuwait City in the final days of the Gulf War, US Marine Corps attack aircraft dropped Gator mines across their path at Mitla Ridge. US attack aircraft then devastated the trapped Iraqi column.

A variation on the cluster bomb theme are dispenser units mounted on aircraft. These allow much larger quantities of more powerful sub-munitions to be carried, but mean that the carrying aircraft has to over-fly the target — giving enemy AA a very easy target. This potentially lethal problem has limited their deployment to just two main systems: the German MW-1 and the British JP.233. USAF chiefs refused to adopt the JP.233 because they considered it a suicide weapon. The

Above: The Belouga dispenser is in widespread use. Operating automatically after release, it carries three different types of submunition—armour-piercing, fragmentation and delayed-action—and a total of 151 bomblets are loaded. Designed for low-level release, the container is retarded by parachute and the submunitions are ejected to cover an area 130ft (40m) wide and either 394ft or 788ft (120m or 240m) long. The spread is selected prior to release of the dispenser.

Right: A JP.233 airfield attack dispenser scatters a mix of 30 SG357 cratering munitions and 215 HB876 area denial mines from a Tornado.

Right: Designed by the German company MBB, this Vertical Ballistic Weapon anti-tank system enables the carrying aircraft to carry out top attacks on armoured targets.

MW-1 can be carried by Alpha Jets or Tornados and is capable of dispensing 4,500 sub-munitions, including 2,250 anti-armour bomblets, 500 anti-tank mines and 650 fragmentation mines.

Dispensers received their combat debut on 17 January 1991, when RAF Tornado GR.1s used the JP.233 for offensive counter-air missions against Iraqi airfields. The weapon had been developed specifically for this type of mission and two sub-munition pods are carried under the hull of a Tornado. Each pod contains 30 SG657 runway-

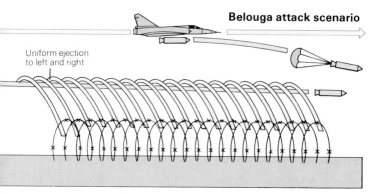

Belouga attack scenario

Uniform ejection
to left and right

VBW *MBB*

cratering bomblets and 215 HB876 area denial mines, which are programmed to explode at random intervals over the 12 hours following delivery to cause casualties among runway repair teams. The optimum attack height is between 50ft (15.2m) and 150ft (45.72m), to ensure a good distribution pattern for the bomblets on the target area. Contrary to popular myth, no Tornado GR.1s were shot down while actually using JP.233s over Iraqi runways, although the crews did report the experience as being pretty scary! Intelligence reports suggest that JP.233 submunitions caused havoc on Iraqi air bases and prevented the Iraqi Air Force from challenging the Coalition air offensive. During the first 24 hours of the war only 118 aircraft of Iraq's 800-strong air force managed to get airborne, with only 24 of them being combat aircraft.

Some targets, such as command bunkers, bridges, communications towers, key structures on industrial sites and hardened aircraft shelters, require precision attacks to ensure destruction, because the blast from a near miss by a "dumb" bomb or a dowsing in cluster sub-munitions has no effect. Laser and computer technologies have been combined to solve this problem.

The main Western laser-guided bomb, or so-called "smart" bomb, in-service is the Texas Instruments Paveway series, which is noted for its simple and cheap design. Paveway bombs are simply standard Mk.82, 83 and 84 series bombs fitted with a laser seeker unit and moveable vanes. A laser designator unit, either ground- or aircraft-mounted, has first to illuminate a target; the seeker unit then adjusts the vanes to guide the bomb towards laser light reflected off the target. Paveway bombs are not missiles and have no rocket motors to assist their flight. This means that launch aircraft have to drop Paveway bombs in much the same way as ordinary bombs and rely on the normal laws of ballistics to get the bomb near

Top right: Locked into a shallow dive, a Canadian Armed Forces CF-18A Hornet ripple fires an underwing pod of 6 CRV-7 2.75in (70mm) aircraft rockets. What it lacks in accuracy the CRV-7 (like other unguided rockets) makes up for as a cheap area denial weapon.

Below: An F-111F banks low over rolling country, showing to good effect the AVQ-26 Pave Tack laser designating pod on its mid-belly, and an underwing load of four Paveway III laser-guided "smart" bombs. Such bombs have been used by F-111Fs against Libya and Iraq.

Delayed lasing

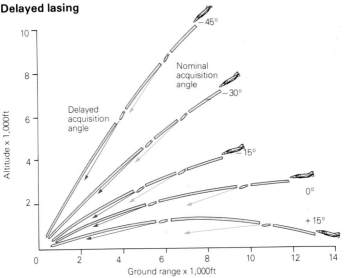

Altitude x 1,000ft

Delayed acquisition angle

Nominal acquisition angle

−45°

−30°

−15°

0°

+15°

Ground range x 1,000ft

Above: Laser guidance demands a fine balance between early and late target acquisition. Early aquisition with shallow trajectory leads to error, as the bomb noses over too soon, but can be overcome by delayed laser illumination.

Laser-guided bomb loft trajectories

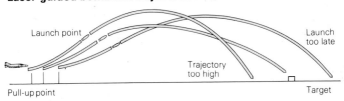

Launch point

Launch too late

Trajectory too high

Pull-up point

Target

Above: Loft bombing with LGB's gives a stand-off capability, but requires the release point, speed, g force and angle to be accuate and ideally an automatic system should be used. The effects of errors are shown here.

to the target. Only then does the laser guidance take over as the bomb drops towards its target.

A whole family of Paveways exist. Paveway I Series bombs use the designation GBU-12 when based on the 500lb (227kg) Mk.82 bomb and GBU-10 when fitted to the 2,000lb (908kg) Mk.84 bombs. The more advanced Paveway III Series bombs, which have larger fins and better seeker units, are termed GBU-22s when fitted to Mk.82 bombs and GBU-24s when fitted to Mk.84s. Due to the small size of the F-117A Stealth fighter's weapons bay, a special version called the GBU-27 was developed which combines the advanced guidance system of the Paveway III Series with the smaller fins of the GBU-10. To enable the GBU-24 and -27 to deal with very heavily-protected targets, so-called "penetrator" versions have been developed which use the I-200 or BL-109/B warhead. To destroy deep Iraqi command bunkers the USAF rushed the GBU-27 into service in February 1991; its 2,000lb (908kg) improved warhead can penetrate 20ft (6m) of concrete or 100ft (30m) of earth. Two were successfully dropped by USAF F-111Fs on a bunker complex at Al Taji near Baghdad on the final day of the Gulf War.

The USAF say that approximately

Above: More advanced than the Paveway family of LGBs, the GBU-15(V) sports either a TV or IR seeker in its nose.

90 per cent of their laser-guided bombs landed on target during the Gulf War, but they are not "wonder weapons" and require great skill and perfect weather conditions to secure a hit. Highly-accurate target intelligence was needed to enable pilots to pin-point their targets at night using sensors. If cloud obscured the target then it could not be successfully designated, and if cloud drifted across the path of a laser beam then the lock would break, causing the bomb to free-fall ballistically. It usually took several minutes for aircraft flying at medium to high altitudes to successfully acquire and then designate targets. While the bomb is dropping to the target the operator of the laser designator has to keep the target illuminated. This procedure requires great concentration by the aircrew, making them very vulnerable to SAMs and other threats.

Slightly more advanced than the Paveway series is the GBU-15(V) 2/B, which has a television or infra-red seeker unit in the nose. Images are relayed to the launch aircraft by data link for corrective instructions. The GBU-15(V) can therefore be launched

Above: Caught on very high speed film, a GBU-15 Modular Guided Weapon System homes in on the target area. The weapon and its 2,000lb (908kg) warhead can be locked onto the target before or after launch for automatic weapon guidance, or it can be manually steered by the Weapon System Operator. The latter is performed via the AN/AXQ-14 two-way data link, which relays visual images to the WSO's TV monitor.

in significantly less benign conditions and allows the launch aircraft to take evasive action immediately after release. The superb accuracy of the weapon was demonstrated on 27 February 1991, when F-111Fs destroyed Iraqi-controlled pumping stations at Mina Al Ahmadi, in Kuwait, that were discharging crude oil into the Arabian Gulf.

Guided missiles give attack aircraft the capability to put ordnance on the target without having to make dangerous bomb runs over or near to the target. Many guided missiles are specially designed for particular missions, such as destroying tanks, ships or radars.

One of the most successful air-to-ground missiles (AGM) is the Hughes AGM-65 Maverick, which saw service on US A-10As, F-16s, AV-8Bs and F-4G Phantom Wild Weasels during the Gulf conflict, scoring an 80 per cent hit rate. The USAF alone fired 5,500 Mavericks, with Iraqi tanks being the main targets. Maverick comes in four main versions, but the television or electro-optical (EO) and imaging infra-red (IIR) versions were the most widely used in the Gulf War. The EO version is locked onto its target by the pilot who locates targets using a television camera in the nose of the missile. Once fired, the Maverick homes automatically onto its target, leaving the pilot free to select further targets or get out of AA range. The IIR version has superior night performance because its infra-red sensors show tanks as "hot spots" at night. The manufacturer's brochure gives the Maverick a range of up to 25 miles (40km) if released at altitude by aircraft flying at Mach 1.2. Combat experience proved that such claims were slightly exaggerated. While the F-16 pilots could locate targets at five miles (8km) range with the Maverick system, it was very difficult to properly identify them and they wasted many missiles on unimportant targets, such as trucks or the hulks of destroyed tanks. The

Right: One of the undoubted success stories in the world of air-to-ground missiles is the AGM-65 Maverick, two of which are on this AV-8B.

Below: Proof of the AGM-65 Maverick missile's "killing" power in the anti-tank role, as experienced by the Iraqi Army during the Gulf War.

slow-flying and armoured A-10As could take the risk of getting close to the enemy's AA fire to make good target selection, but the more fragile F-16s had to stay at safer distances and so were unable to use the Maverick to its full potential.

The range of AGMs is steadily being increased to give better stand-off capability and hence better protection for launch aircraft. In this area, naval weapons are some of the most advanced because of the great distances involved in maritime warfare. Compared to the cluttered land battlefield, the sea provides ships with very little protection from surveillance systems such as radar or thermal imaging. Miniaturised radars can now be fitted into the noses of missiles, such as the McDonnell Douglas AGM-84 Harpoon, Aerospatiale AM.39 Exocet, British Aerospace Sea Skua and Sea Eagle, Kongsberg Penguin and MBB Kormoran. They approach their targets only a few feet above the waves to avoid detection by enemy radar and only illuminate their targets with radar for confirmation of final guidance data. Computer data links also enable friendly surveillance aircraft to pass targeting intelligence to the missiles in flight.

Targets can be hit at ranges from 9.3 miles (15km) for the Sea Skua to 75 miles (120km) for the Harpoon. Exocet missiles showed the effectiveness of modern guided missiles during the Falklands War and the Iran-Iraq "tanker" war in the Arabian Gulf. Exocet hits, however, rarely proved fatal because of the small size of the missile's warhead. Ships only tended to be lost if poor firefighting drills or equipment allowed the resulting fires to get out of control.

A hybrid of the Harpoon missile is the McDonnell Douglas AGM-84E Stand-off Land Attack Missile, which combines the Harpoon's body with the Maverick IIR seeker rather than a radar set. A data link relays images from the seeker unit back to the control aircraft. Seven were fired against Iraqi land targets during the Gulf War from US Navy strike aircraft, from ranges of up to 60 nautical miles (111km). Good hits with each missile were recorded by operators who literally "flew" the missiles into the doors of Iraqi factories.

Right: Anti-shipping missiles tend to be large, like this AM.39 Exocet being launched by a Mirage F.1. The target is acquired at long distance by radar, and the coordinates are fed into the missile's inertial navigation system for the mid-course sector; terminal homing is by active radar.

Below: Derived from a surface-to-surface missile, Penguin 3 can be carried by the F-16 as seen here. It can fly a dogleg course if programmed to do so, and uses infra-red terminal homing, which does not betray its presence with an emission and therefore cannot be effectively jammed.

Radar revolutionised air warfare in World War Two when the RAF used it to give vital early warning of Luftwaffe attacks. In less than 20 years, scientists had turned the tables on radars and developed missiles that homed in on their electronic emissions. Today's anti-radar or anti-radiation missiles are very, very sophisticated and enable attack aircraft to make life very unhealthy for enemy air defences.

Suppression of Enemy Air Defence (SEAD), or anti-radar missions are a deadly "cat and mouse" game between radar or SAM missile operators and attack aircraft that are trying to put them out of business. Early anti-radiation missiles, such as the Texas Instruments AGM-45A Shrike, lacked the speed and flexibility to enable them to hit home before enemy radar operators realised they were under attack and swtiched off their sets or jumped frequency. Modern missiles, such as the Texas Instruments AGM-88A High Speed Anti-Radiation Missile (HARM) or British Aerospace Air-Launched Anti-Radar Missile (ALARM), were developed to give the SEAD aircraft the edge they needed to escort attack aircraft safely to their targets. More than 1,000 HARMs were fired during the Gulf War and the USAF and US Navy's SEAD campaign resulted in the Iraqi's effectively switching their radars off from Day 2 of the war. HARMs proved effective in pre-programmed or "range unknown" modes, where the coordinates and frequency details of known radars are fed into the missile before take-off, or where target information is fed into the HARM in-flight from an accompanying F-4G Wild Weasel that locates an enemy radar with its APR-47 radar detection system. In the Gulf War this combination worked with devastating effect. The HARM's Mach 2 speed meant it was able to strike its target before many Iraqi radar operators had the faintest idea that a missile was heading their way.

Increasingly, attack aircraft are being equipped with high-technology sensor equipment to enable their weapons to be delivered with great accuracy in all weathers and at night.

Below: A German Navy Tornado carrying four AGM-88A HARM anti-radiation missiles and two ALQ-119 jamming pods.

Alarm indirect attack mode

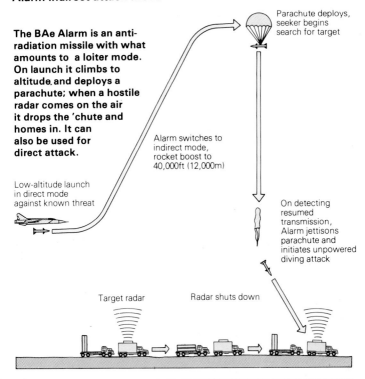

The BAe Alarm is an anti-radiation missile with what amounts to a loiter mode. On launch it climbs to altitude and deploys a parachute; when a hostile radar comes on the air it drops the 'chute and homes in. It can also be used for direct attack.

Parachute deploys, seeker begins search for target

Low-altitude launch in direct mode against known threat

Alarm switches to indirect mode, rocket boost to 40,000ft (12,000m)

On detecting resumed transmission, Alarm jettisons parachute and initiates unpowered diving attack

Target radar   Radar shuts down

Thermal imaging (TI) or Forward Looking Infra-Red (FLIR) technology uses computers to turn infra-red radiation into images similar to television pictures. Current systems, such as LANTIRN, provide imagery that is good enough to allow attack aircraft to fly safely at low level, at night. These systems, when linked up to a laser designator such as the AVQ-23 PAVE SPIKE or AVQ-26 PAVE TACK, allow "smart" bombs to be targeted at night. The crystal-clear television pictures of laser-guided bombs in action from the Gulf War were all recorded from TI/FLIR sensors.

Targeting radars provide vital information for aircraft without TI, operating at night or in bad weather. Modern terrain-following radar provides aircrews with virtual maps of the ground ahead, showing hills, rivers, buildings and other prominent features, which are accurate enough to bomb by. Many US aircraft are now fitted with NAVSTAR Global Positioning System (GPS) terminals to allow crews to receive navigation information from orbiting satellites. GPS was used with great success during the Gulf War.

Below: The white pod visible beneath the fuselage of this RAF Tornado GR.1 is a Thermal Imaging Airborne Laser Designator (TIALD), pod, as used during the Gulf War.

Left: The underwing AGM-88A HARM anti-radiation missiles identify the anti-radar role of the F-4G/F-16C Wild Weasel airborne hunter-killer team.

Prowlers and EC-130H Compass Call aircraft all saw service over Iraq in the Gulf War to great effect. Crews of Compass Call aircraft, for example, specialised in listening out for Iraqi air defence controllers and then jammed their radios with "heavy metal" music whenever they tried to order attacks on coalition aircraft.

"The bomber will always get through" was the catch phrase of air power enthusiasts in the 1930s. Increasingly that phrase began to ring hollow after the success of Soviet-made SAMs in Vietnam and the 1973 Yom Kippur War. Starting in the late 1960s, the USAF began a highly-secret programme to produce an attack aircraft that was invisible to radar. It came to fruition in the F-117A Stealth Fighter, which received so much attention during the Gulf War. The USAF officially terms stealth as "low observable" technology and denies that it makes the F-117A totally "invisible" to radar. Very precise flight profiles have to be followed to make the F-117A radar absorbent material and radar signal diffusing shape work to their best effect.

Stealth technology is still in its infancy. To date, the F-117 is the only

Anti-radiation missiles are not the only systems available to attack aircraft to protect them from enemy air defences. Most modern attack aircraft are fitted with radar warning receivers that alert aircrew when their aircraft is being illuminated by radar(s), or is being locked onto by an enemy SAM or air-to-air missile. With suitable warning pilots can let off chaff (strips of alluminium) or flares to deceive radar-guided or heat-seeking missiles respectively. Some aircraft have internal jammers or can carry jamming pods on their weapons pylons. The USAF, US Navy and Luftwaffe have purpose-built jamming aircraft to accompany attack aircraft into battle. US EF-111A Ravens, EA-6B

Below: The F-15E Strike Eagle carries its two Low Altitude Navigation and Targeting by Infra-Red at Night (LANTIRN) pods on pylons located under the aircraft's air intakes.

Above: Developed from the A-6 Intruder, the four-man EA-6B Prowler can jam all emitters operating in a typical air defence complex.

Below: Like the Prowler, the EF-111A Raven can trace its heritage back to another US attack aircraft, namely the F-111A. Transmitters for the

ALGQ-99E Tactical Jamming System are located in the underfuselage "canoe", while the receivers and antennae are in the fin-top fairing.

Above: One of the German Air Force's 35 Tornado ECRs, as used in the electronic combat and reconnaissance role. Note the HARM anti-radar missiles.

frontline aircraft that employs stealth technology to the full. Over the coming years, however, the technology will become a standard feature of attack aircraft and increase greatly their ability to attack heavily-defended enemy positions.

As its combat record in the Gulf War showed, the F-117A is probably the most effective manned penetrator currently in service when it comes to the tactical strike mission. In terms of radar penetration, the F-117A has met its specifications, but at a price of restricted speed and manoeuvrability. No doubt its successors, such as the Lockheed F-22A Superstar (winner of the USAF's Advanced Tactical Fighter fly-off) will combine stealth with an improvement in overall speed, altitude and manoeuvrability.

Above: Deep inside its Hardened Aircraft Shelter (HAS), one of the USAF's 50-odd F-117A Stealth Fighters awaits the call to action during the war with Iraq in 1991.

Right: Forward visibility for the F-117A pilot is limited to say the least. The cavity just ahead of the canopy houses an optical turret for one of the Stealth Fighter's two onboard FLIR systems.

Below: Though relatively few in number, making up 2.5% of USAF air assets deployed in the Gulf, F-117As accounted for over 40% of enemy targets destroyed during the war.

Nanchang Q-5/A-5 Fantan

Type: Twin-engined single-seat close air support and battlefield interdiction aircraft with limited air superiority capability. The Q prefix denotes the Chinese service aircraft while the A prefix indicates the export models.

Only recently has any firm information on the Nanchang Q-5/A-5 come to light as a result of China exploring the export market. It was known that it had been developed from the F-6

fighter, which in turn was a Chinese copy of the Russian MiG-19: what came as a surprise was the age of the project, the prototype having made its first flight as far back as June 1965, rather than 1972 as had been commonly supposed.

The MiG-19/J-6 Farmer was a highly swept design — about 60° on the leading edge — that was long on thrust and short on fuel. Dating back to 1953, it was the first service aircraft to have a thrust/weight ratio nudging

Dimensions	A-5III	A-5M
Length (ft/m)	50.58/15.42	50.58/15.42
Span (ft/m)	31.83/9.70	31.83/9.70
Height (ft/m)	14.82/4.52	14.82/4.52
Wing area (sq ft/m²)	301/27.95	301/27.95
Aspect ratio	3.37	3.37
Weights		
Empty (lb/kg)	14,316/6,494	14,625/6,634
Clean takeoff (lb/kg)	21,553/9,776	21,863/9,917
Max takeoff (lb/kg)	26,450/12,000	26,450/12,000
Max external load (lb/kg)	4,480/2,032	4,480/2,032
Hardpoints	8	8
Power	2 x WP-6 tj	2 x WP-6A tj
Max (lb st/kN)	7,165/31.8	8,267/36.7
Mil (lb st/kN)	5,730/25.5	6,614/29.4
Fuel		
Internal (lb/kg)	6,353/2,882	6,353/2,882
External (lb/kg)	3,984/1,807	3,984/1,807
Fraction	0.29	0.29
Loadings		
Max thrust	0.66 − 0.54	0.76 − 0.63
Mil thrust	0.53 − 0.43	0.61 − 0.50
Wing clean to (lb/sq ft/kg/m²)	72/350	73/355
Wing max to (lb/sq ft/kg/m²)	88/429	88/429
Performance		
Vmax hi	M = 1.12	M = 1.20
Vmax lo	M = 0.99	M = 1.00
Ceiling (ft/m)	52,000/15,850	52,500/16,000
Initial climb (ft/min/m/sec)	N/A	N/A
Takeoff roll (ft/m)	4,100/1,250	3,940/1,200
Landing roll (ft/m)	3,480/1,060	3,480/1,060
First flight	5 June 1965 (prototype)	

unity at combat weight, and as such it was almost two decades ahead of its time, but the Soviet Union quickly junked it in favour of the Mach 2-capable MiG-21.

The Q-5/A-5 Fantan has already appeared in three versions and is about to emerge in a fourth. Ordnance could be hung externally on the J-6 Farmer, but the resulting drag would restrict the operational radius of a fighter already handicapped by the very low fuel fraction of 0.22. The Chinese answer was to redesign it to accommodate an internal weapons bay, and as the F-6 was already a tight piece of packaging it was decided to extend the fuselage in length and perform an extensive rhinoplasty operation,

deleting the simple pitot intake of the fighter in favour of two side intakes. These considerable structural changes increased the weight, and the wings were enlarged by just less than 8 per cent in span and 12 per cent in area. The flaps were redesigned and the underwing spoilers omitted, while the area of the vertical tail was increased and the 30mm cannon was replaced by 23mm cannon.

The main version in service with the People's Liberation Army Air Force is designated the Q-5III. Some 150 are to be purchased by the Pakistan Air Force under the designation A-5C. They feature a number of "westernisation" modifications including Martin-Baker Mk.10 zero-zero ejection seats and fittings for AIM-9P Sidewinder air-to-air missiles.

Co-operation agreements have been made with the Italian Aeritalia firm to upgrade the Q-5 to A-5M standard by fitting a new ranging radar, internal navigation system, a new head-up display and extra underwing weapons pylons.

Users
China, North Korea, Pakistan

Left: The Fantan also carries out the maritime strike role armed with two C-801 air-to-surface anti-shipping missiles.

Below: A Q-5 II of the Chinese Air Force with a respectable array of stores visible on no less than 10 stations.

Dassault-Breguet Mirage F.1

Type: Single-seat single-engined multi-role fighter and attack aircraft. Variants include reconnaissance and two-seat training types.

The limitations of the delta-winged Mirage III/5/50 series were an unnecessarily high takeoff and landing speed with correspondingly long

Dimensions	Mirage F.1E
Length (ft/m)	50.00/15.24
Span (ft/m)	27.58/8.41
Height (ft/m)	14.75/4.50
Wing area (sq ft/m²)	269/25.00
Aspect ratio	2.83

Weights	
Empty (lb/kg)	16,315/7,400
Clean takeoff (lb/kg)	24,030/10,900
Max takeoff (lb/kg)	35,700/16,200
Max external load (lb/kg)	12,786/5,800
Hardpoints	5

Power	1 x Atar 9K50 tj
Max (lb st/kN)	15,870/70.5
Mil (lb st/kN)	11,060/49.0

Fuel	
Internal (lb/kg)	7,384/3,350
External (lb/kg)	7,540/3,420
Fraction	0.31

Loadings	
Max thrust	0.66 – 0.44
Mil thrust	0.46 – 0.31
Wing clean to (lb/sq ft/kg/m²)	89/436
Wing max to (lb/sq ft/kg/m²)	133/648

Performance	
Vmax hi	M = 2.2
Vmax lo	M = 1.2
Ceiling (ft/m)	65,000/22,000
Initial climb (ft/min/m/sec)	41,930/213
Takeoff roll (ft/m)	1,968/600
Landing roll (ft/m)	2,198/670

First flight	Dec 1966 (prototype)

ground rolls, high energy loss during hard manoeuvring and, more important in the attack role, a very bumpy ride at high speed and low levels which, if sustained for more a than few minutes, lowered crew efficiency. After a brief flirtation with variable-sweep wings on the Mirage G and G8, which seemed to be very capable aeroplanes, France then decided that its real requirement was for a Mach 3 interceptor with fixed wings. The requirement for the *Avion de Combat Futur* changed radically between 1972 and 1975, and hardware finally emerged as the Mirage F.2, a two-seat all-weather fighter powered by the American TF30 turbofan. Meanwhile, Dassault had built a single-seat version which was scaled down and wrapped around the current French engine, the Atar 9K. This was preferred to the larger F.2, and was ordered in quantity as the F.1, at first to fill the air interception role.

The Mirage F.1 had, in numerical terms, a performance comparable to that of the Mirage 3, but its orthodox layout, coupled with full-span leading edge flaps and double-slotted trailing edge flaps to the wings, reduced runway requirements and improved turning capability, while the wings' small lifting area and consequent high loading, combined with a modest aspect ratio to give a low gust response, resulted in a smooth ride at high speed and low level, which suited the aircraft well to the attack mission.

The Mirage F.1A, which has ceased production, was optimised for the attack mission, with the Système d'Attaque au Sol (SAS) using the AIDA 2 radar in place of the Cyrano IV of the air superiority version giving an extremely good first-pass strike capability at low level. The Mirage F.1B and D are two-seat training versions of the F-1C and E respectively, the F-1C being optimised for the interception and air superiority roles while the F-1E is a true multi-role aircraft, being fitted with a modern nav/attack system which includes extra modes to the Cyrano IV radar to give continuously computed air-to-ground ranging, penetration contour mapping, supplementary radar navigation functions and blind let down. These are combined with the SAGEM ULISS 47 INS, new digital computers and HUD to give greater attack accuracy, and digital panels for stores management and navigation to ease significantly the pilot's mission workload.

Iraq was the main export customer for the Mirage F.1, with more than 100 aircraft of various versions being supplied to Saddam Hussein's air force in the mid-1980s. They proved effective in the anti-shipping role with AM.39 Exocet missiles during the Iran-Iraq War, but were outmatched by US F-15 Eagles during the Gulf War.

Eight were lost to the F-15s in air-to-air combat. Another five were captured on the ground by Coalition troops and 24 were flown to Iran where they were confiscated against that country's claim for reparations during the Iran-Iraq war — including shipping losses incurred as a result of attacks by Mirage F.1s.

French Mirage F.1CRs and those of Arab Coalition allies were grounded for the first phase of Operation *Desert Storm* because of the danger of being mistaken for Iraqi aircraft. Once Coalition air supremacy was assured they performed well in reconnaissance and ground attack roles.

Users
Ecuador, France, Greece, Iraq, Jordan, Kuwait, Libya, Morocco, Qatar, South Africa, Spain

Above: An aweome display of firepower as a Mirage F.1 fires all four Sneb rocket pods at once.

Below: Mirage F.1s drop their BAT 120 retarded bombs over a simulated armoured column.

Dassault-Breguet Mirage 2000N

Type: Two-seat single-engined nuclear strike/attack aircraft. Other variants are the 2000C single-seat interceptor/air superiority fighter with multi-role capability, including air-to-ground; the 2000B two-seat conversion trainer; and the 2000R reconnaissance aircraft. Export models have other designations.

The Mirage 2000 resulted from an Armée de l'Air requirement for a multi-role fighter capable of intercepting very high-speed, high-altitude intruders; it was also to replace the elderly Mirage III and the Mirage F.1. The maximum speed of Mach 3 originally specified was gradually lowered to Mach 2.7, and then still further reduced. Two factors influenced the relaxation of the top speed requirement; cost was certainly one, as the proposed new fighter would have been some two and a half times as expensive as the Mirage F.1 to procure; the other was the projected performance of the next generation of missiles.

Dimensions	Mirage 2000N
Length (ft/m)	46.50/14.17
Span (ft/m)	29.50/8.99
Height (ft/m)	N/A
Wing area (sq ft/m²)	441/40.98
Aspect ratio	1.97

Weights	
Empty (lb/kg)	17,000/7,710
Clean takeoff (lb/kg)	23,750/10,773
Max takeoff (lb/kg)	36,375/16,500
Max external load (lb/kg)	16,755/7,600
Hardpoints	9

Power	1 x SNECMA M53-P2 tf
Max (lb st/kN)	21,400/95.0
Mil (lb st/kN)	14,400/64.0

Fuel	
Internal (lb/kg)	6,346/2,880
External (lb/kg)	8,758/3,973
Fraction	0.27

Loadings	
Max thrust	0.90 − 0.59
Mil thrust	0.61 − 0.40
Wing clean to (lb/sq ft/kg/m²)	54/263
Wing max to (lb/sq ft/kg/m²)	82/403

Performance	
Vmax hi	M = 2.35
Vmax lo	M = 1.20
Ceiling (ft/m)	60,000/18,300
Initial climb (ft/min/m/sec)	49,212/250
Takeoff roll (ft/m)	N/A
Landing roll (ft/m)	1,200/410

First flight	20 Nov 1982

At the time that the Super Mirage was cancelled, Dassault were working on a simpler and cheaper aircraft, the Mirage 2000, a reversion to the simple delta wing of the Mirage III, which had been superseded by the more orthodox tailed Mirage F.1. The delta layout had been well suited to high-speed, high-altitude flight, but had certain disadvantages in manoeuvre combat. However, the advent of relaxed static stability combined with quadruplex fly-by-wire could produce a very manoeuvrable fighter which retained the high-speed, high-altitude advantages of the delta planform. Variable camber also helped, the full-span leading edge slats operating automatically as a function of angle of attack when the undercarriage was up, and combining with two-section elevons to the entire trailing edge. Small strakes were fitted to the sides of the engine inlets to produce a vortex, and to reduce the download. And to offset the limited power available, composite materials were used extensively to reduce weight.

The result was a small, fast and highly manoeuvrable fighter with a good rate of climb, and one which was affordable in the sort of quantities that made sense, making it an attractive proposition in the export market. For the attack role a total of

Below: A fine portrait of the Mirage 2000N's "coke bottle" fuselage and large delta wing.

nine hardpoints were built in, although two of these have a limit of 660lb (300kg) and four more are limited to 880lb (400kg), leaving only three with a heavy load capability — some 3,970lb (1,800kg). While other stores can be carried, the lighter-rated hardpoints are generally used for AAMs or equipment pods, depending on the needs of the specific mission. Two 30mm DEFA 554 cannon with 125 rounds of ammunition each are installed internally.

The Thomson-CSF RDM multimode radar has, in addition to its air-to-air modes, certain air-to-ground functions, namely ground mapping, contour mapping, terrain avoidance, air-to-ground ranging and sea search and track; coupled with a state of the art nav/attack system and an internal ECM suite, it provides a very fair air-to-ground capability.

The Mirage 2000N has a two-man crew and is based on the 2000B two seat conversion trainer. In place of the RDF radar, it has the ESD/THCSF Antipole radar with a terrain-following mode, optimised for air-to-ground weapons delivery and deep penetration at low level in darkness or adverse weather. This allows automatic flight at 300ft (90m) above ground level, to be reduced to 200ft (60m) in future,

and is coupled with a SAGEM INS and a comprehensive avionics suite which allows first-pass blind strikes to be made on pre-targeted points.

In the nuclear strike role the main weapon will be the ASMP stand-off missile, which has a 150kT warhead, carried on the centreline.

French Mirage 2000C's of the 5*eme* Escadre de Chasses flew 508 air defence sorties and 1,416 combat hours during the Gulf War. The first of 14 aircraft arrived at Al Ahsa in Saudi Arabia in October 1990. They were used exclusively for air defence, as were the Mirage 2000EADs of the United Arab Emirates Air Force.

The French aircraft featured the new Radar Doppler et Impulsion radar, which were upgraded to S4-1/S4-2 standard. New chaff/flare dispensers had also been fitted beneath their rear fuselages. Their usual warload was four Super 530D beyond visual range and two Matra Magic 2 heat-seeking air-to-air missiles.

Users
Abu Dhabi, Egypt, France, Greece, India, Peru

Below: A French Air Force Mirage 2000N carrying an ASMP missile on the centreline.

Dassault-Breguet Super Etendard

Type: Single-seat single-engined carrier-based strike fighter with limited air-to-air capability.

The Super Etendard began life as a cheap upgrade of the Etendard IVM with improved avionics and a wing modified to give better performance, while the more powerful Atar 8K50 replaced the Atar 8C. In the event,

Dimensions	Super Etendard
Length (ft/m)	46.96/14.31
Span (ft/m)	31.48/9.59
Height (ft/m)	12.67/3.86
Wing area (sq ft/m²)	306/28.41
Aspect ratio	3.24

Weights	
Empty (lb/kg)	14,330/6,500
Clean takeoff (lb/kg)	20,833/9,450
Max takeoff (lb/kg)	26,455/12,000
Max external load (lb/kg)	4,630/2,100
Hardpoints	5

Power	1 x Atar 9K50 tj
Max (lb st/kN)	N/A
Mil (lb st/kN)	11,025/49.0

Fuel	
Internal (lb/kg)	6,800/3,084
External (lb/kg)	4,800/2,180
Fraction	0.33

Loadings	
Max thrust	N/A
Mil thrust	0.53 – 0.42
Wing clean to (lb/sq ft/kg/m²)	68/333
Wing max to (lb/sq ft/kg/m²)	87/423

Performance	
Vmax hi	M = 1.00
Vmax lo	M = 0.96
Ceiling (ft/m)	45,000/13,700
Initial climb (ft/min/m/sec)	24,600/125
Takeoff roll (ft/m)	N/A
Landing roll (ft/m)	N/A

First flight	28 Oct 1974

the Super Etendard emerged as an almost new aeroplane, albeit with a marked family resemblance to the IVM. The main differences are the wing, which has drooping leading edge and double slotted trailing edge flaps, the 8K50 Atar engine, the Thomson CSF/ESD Agave radar optimised for naval missions and a comprehensive nav/attack system.

The official roles of the Super Etendard are given as fleet protection against attack from surface vessels, ground attack, photo-reconnaissance, and fleet air defence, not necessarily in that order. The fleet air defence mission is necessarily of a limited nature; the Super Etendard hardly compares with an F-14, but closely approximates the Sea Harrier in the pursuit and destruction of shadowers such as the Tu-20 Bear, carrying two R550 Magic missiles on the outboard pylons and two 30mm DEFA cannon mounted internally with 125 rounds each.

Super Etendard, with its subsonic performance and unexceptional

appearance, was built in small numbers, some 85 in all, and unlike the majority of Dassault-Breguet aircraft made little impact on the export market.

The Super Etendard first achieved prominence in the South Atlantic in 1982 in Argentinian Navy service. A total of four aircraft were serviceable out of five delivered and five Exocets were available: 12 sorties were flown, and all five missiles were launched, resulting in the destruction of HMS *Sheffield* and MV *Atlantic Conveyor*. An element of luck played a part in both these sinkings; *Sheffield* was caught with her defences down, while the *Atlantic Conveyor* was hit by a missile decoyed away from the warships. It is tempting to speculate on the outcome had the old *Ark Royal*, with Gannet AEW aircraft and Phantom fighters, been present.

Super Etendards were next in action over the Lebanon in September 1983, in support of the French contingent of the peace-keeping force; operating from *Foch* and, later, from *Clemenceau*, they provided air support over the subsequent few months.

The next nation to operate the Super Etendard was Iraq, to which a batch of five was supplied, apparently on a sale or return basis pending the delivery of Exocet-compatible Mirage F.1EQ-5s. Details are sparse, but the first operation took place on March 27, 1984. A considerable number of ships have been damaged, but few have sunk and none can definitely be attributed to the Super Etendard. The surviving aircraft (one is believed lost) returned to France early in 1985.

In French service the Super Etendard provides the Aéronavale with a nuclear strike capability carrying the AN-52, which will be replaced by the stand-off ASMP in the 1990s.

The Super Etendard is now getting very old, with its performance and avionics being inferior to modern American carrier-borne strike aircraft. Cost reasons may force the Aéronavale to turn to up-dated versions of the McDonnel-Douglas F/A-18 Hornet to equip its new generation of nuclear-powered carriers, as an extremely urgent "stop-gap" until the arrival of the Dassault-Breguet Rafale M in service.

Users
Argentina, France

Below: A rocket pod-armed Super Etendard prepares to launch from a carrier.

Aeritalia/Aermacchi/ EMBRAER AMX

Type: Single-seat single-engined multi-role aircraft with the accent on attack but with some air-to-air and reconnaissance capability. Two-seat variants are proposed for advanced training, anti-shipping, and electronic warfare.

Design studies for AMX began in 1977, the objective being an aircraft to replace the Fiat G.91 in the light attack and reconnaissance roles and the F-104 in both those roles plus counter-air and anti-shipping attack.

A consortium set up between Aeritalia and Aermacchi was later joined by Embraer of Brazil, whose air arm wanted a comparable machine. Although firm orders have been placed by both Italy and Brazil, and other countries have been reported as showing interest, AMX appears to be ploughing a lonely furrow. Nowhere else has a firmly subsonic dedicated attack machine been developed from scratch, nor are AMX's baseline performance figures anything startling. In the international marketplace it is

Dimensions	AMX
Length (ft/m)	44.52/13.57
Span (ft/m)	29.10/8.87
Height (ft/m)	14.99/4.57
Wing area (sq ft/m²)	226/21.00
Aspect ratio	3.75

Weights	
Empty (lb/kg)	14,771/6,700
Clean takeoff (lb/kg)	21,164/9,600
Max takeoff (lb/kg)	27,558/12,500
Max external load (lb/kg)	8,377/3,800
Hardpoints	5

Power	1 x Spey RB168-807 tf
Max (lb st/kN)	N/A
Mil (lb st/kN)	11,000/49.0

Fuel	
Internal (lb/kg)	6,000/2,720
External (lb/kg)	N/A
Fraction	0.28

Loadings	
Max thrust	N/A
Mil thrust	0.52 − 0.40
Wing clean to (lb/sq ft/kg/m²)	94/457
Wing max to (lb/sq ft/kg/m²)	122/595

Performance	
Vmax hi	N/A
Vmax lo	M = 0.86
Ceiling (ft/m)	42,650/13,000
Initial climb (ft/min/m/sec)	Not released
Takeoff roll (ft/m)	2,460/750
Landing roll (ft/m)	N/A

First flight	May 1983

competing both with refurbished old designs upgraded with advanced avionics fits and with adapted and armed advanced trainers, both of which are going to work out much cheaper than AMX, which is quite a large aircraft for its payload/range performance.

Little firm information has been released about the avionics fit, but it is known that an advanced nav/attack system has been tailored around two main computers via a digital data bus, while plenty of space exists to allow extra systems to be fitted as necessary; an internal ECM suite is carried, incorporating RWR and both active jammers and expendables. For reconnaissance missions pallet-mounted photographic systems can be loaded, or an infra red/optronics pod can be hung on the centreline. The Brazilian and Italian aircraft differ in weaponry: the latter have a single 20mm M61 Vulcan cannon mounted internally, whereas the Brazilians have been forced by US export restrictions to mount two 30mm DEFA cannon.

AMX (the name has yet to be decided but it has to mean the same in both Italian and Portuguese) has been designed to haul a moderate load out of a short or semi-prepared airfield, and take it a moderate distance at high subsonic speed and

Below: The first of 79 AMXs due to enter service with the Brazilian Air Force by 1994.

low level, by day or by night, and in less than perfect weather conditions. Forecasts have been made that there is a large market for the anti-shipping variant "with practically no opposition". If that means there is little opposition from purpose-made aircraft, the statement is correct, but in practice there are many fighters and even more armed trainers that can carry specialised anti-ship missiles such as Exocet, Sea Eagle, Kormoran or Harpoon. In fact, it would be a singularly small or ill-equipped aircraft that could not be fitted out to both carry and launch at least one of these types of anti-ship missiles.

Comparisons are odious, but difficult to avoid in the case of AMX and Hawk 200. The British aircraft carries 18 per cent less rather faster, and using a hi-lo-lo-hi profile, for considerably further than the AMX; using a lo-lo profile the gap is substantially reduced but still exists. Hawk 200 has better short-field performance, and is far superior in air-combat should it have to fight its way home, and while the licence-built Spey in the AMX gives considerably more thrust, the heavier weight of the bigger machine makes the difference between the respective thrust loadings mariginal. At the bottom line, weight equates roughly with cost, and AMX is some 6,000lb (2,725kg) or 69 per cent heavier than the Hawk, which, on a strict knock for knock basis, would mean five Hawk 200s for the price of three AMXs. An even more attractive option would be to acquire the Hawk 60 series and add advanced pilot training to its list of operational roles.

On the other hand, AMX is large enough to accommodate considerable growth in terms of avionics systems and has been designed with a surplus of power in both electric and hydraulic systems, although the two-seat version will lose one fuselage fuel tank, which will reduce its range and endurance.

Carrying an external load of 6,000lb (2,720kg), with a gross take-off weight, AMX has an attack radius of 280nm (520km) usiing a hi-lo-lo-hi profile, while in the lo-lo mission at the same weights the figures decrease to some 200nm (370km).

The Italian Air Force took delivery of the first of 136 AMXs in October 1989. 103° Gruppo of 51° Stormo at Istrana and six further squadrons are to be formed for light attack, reconnaissance and anti-shipping missions. Some 95 AMXs are to be purchased by the Brazilian Air Force and deliveries also began in 1989. The Brazilians plan to form five AMX-equipped squadrons. Budgetary problems in this South American country are likely to restrict plans to buy up to 150 aircraft.

Refuelling trials have taken place from Brazilian KC-130 and KC-707 tankers, as well as Italian Air Force Tornados using "buddy" packs. Nicknamed the "pocket Tornado", the AMX is proving to be a very successful aircraft. Export prospects for what is a relatively cheap weapons platform with much potential look promising. Several smaller air arms, are being courted for orders.

Users
Brazil, Italy

Above: An AMX of 51° Stormo, Italian Air Force, the initial operational AMX unit.

Below: An Italian AMX displays its four underwing and single fuselage hardpoints.

Dassault-Breguet/ Dornier Alpha Jet

Type: Two-seat twin-engined armed trainer/light attack aircraft. Variants include the Alpha Jet NGEA (Nouvelle Generation Ecole-Appui), the Alpha Jet Lancier for close suport and anti-shipping operations, and a Dornier-developed advanced trainer with a state of the art cockpit.

The Alpha Jet was designed to meet

Dimensions	Alpha Jet NGEA
Length (ft/m)	43.42/13.23
Span (ft/m)	29.92/9.12
Height (ft/m)	13.75/4.19
Wing area (sq ft/m²)	188/17.50
Aspect ratio	4.75

Weights	
Empty (lb/kg)	7,749/3,515
Clean takeoff (lb/kg)	11,398/5,170
Max takeoff (lb/kg)	17,637/8,000
Max external load (lb/kg)	5,510/2,500
Hardpoints	4

Power	2 x Larzac 04 C20 tf
Max (lb st/kN)	N/A
Mil (lb st/kN)	3,175/14.1

Fuel	
Internal (lb/kg)	3,648/1,655
External (lb/kg)	3,174/1,440
Fraction	0.32

Loadings	
Max thrust	N/A
Mil thrust	0.56 − 0.36
Wing clean to (lb/sq ft/kg/m²)	60/295
Wing max to (lb/sq ft/kg/m²)	94/457

Performance	
Vmax hi	M = 0.86
Vmax lo	M = 0.85
Ceiling (ft/m)	48,000/14,600
Initial climb (ft/min/m/sec)	11,220/57
Takeoff roll (ft/m)	1,345/410
Landing roll (ft/m)	2,000/610

First flight	April 1982

a joint need by France and Germany for an advanced trainer, while Germany also needed a light attack/reconnaissance aircraft to replace its ageing Fiat G.91s. The dual requirement was not incompatible — almost any aircraft has some weapons carrying capability, and an advanced trainer more than most — and it is economic sense to operate a dual-role trainer/attack aircraft to increase force size in time of war, although the Armée de l'Air were to use the Alpha Jet purely in the training role, while the Luftaffe intention was to use it operationally with the rear seat removed.

The two seats were set in tandem, with the rear one raised to give the back-seat pilot a good view over the front seater's head. Two small Larzac turbofans were adopted to give twin-engine safety, and a short though sturdy undercarriage, capable of grass field operation, was used, a feature which necessitated the use of a shoulder-mounted wing to give sufficient clearance for a wide variety of stores to be carried. Clearance beneath the fuselage was too little for much other than a gun pod, a 30mm DEFA cannon being carried by the French aircraft and a 27mm Mauser by the German, each with 125 rounds.

As might be expected, the avionics fit on the Luftwaffe Alpha Jets was more comprehensive than that on their French counterparts; apart from the usual communications gear, ILS, Tacan and IFF, a simple computerised weapon aiming sight is carried, while the German aircraft features a HUD, radio altimeter, Doppler velocity sensors and navigation equipment and a far more sophisticated weapons release system. It has a pitot probe, and a more pointed nose than the French trainer, while the Alpha Jets dedicated to the attack role have no duplicated controls in the rear cockpit; instead they carry various items of ECM gear on the seat bearers. The nose shape is the main external difference btween the two, but the French aircraft also feature narrow strakes on the sides of the nose to improve spin resistance.

The next development, the Alpha Jet NGEA, is fitted with a much more capable nav/attack system and has a chisel nose with a laser ranger, a more accurate INS, and a HUD, coupled with the features already adopted by the Luftwaffe machine. Five attack modes are possible, including offset bombing.

The shortage of hardpoints makes it unlikely that the Alpha Jet would carry drop tanks in war as it would lose half its load-carrying capacity at a stroke, but with a good fuel fraction and economical turbofans its payload/range is perfectly adequate for its task: in the close air support mission, flown with six 550lb (250kg) retarded bombs and the gun pod, it has a loiter time of 35 minutes at a radius of 110nm (200m) using an all-lo profile, while the same sortie with no loiter time could extend to a radius of 205nm (380km) in a lo-lo profile or 305nm (565km) using a hi-lo-lo-hi profile.

The Luftwaffe deployed 18 Alpha Jet As of Jagdbombergeschwader (JBG: Fighter Bomber Wing) 43, based at Oldenburg, to Erhac in Turkey as part of the NATO Allied Command Europe's Mobile Force, in January 1991. This force was intended to defend Turkey in the event of an Iraqi attack but in the end was not involved in any combat.

As part of German defence cuts announced in the summer of 1991, the Luftwaffe is to retire its 175 Alpha Jets from service by 1993 when JBG 41, 43 and 49 are disbanded. Some may be retained for training roles and others transferred to the Portuguese Air Force.

Users
Belgium, Cameroon, Egypt, France, Germany, Ivory Coast, Morocco, Nigeria, Qatar, Togo

Below: The Luftwaffe uses the Alpha Jet A (175 of which were procured) primarily in the close air support role. Note the centreline gun pack.

Below: Formerly known as the Alpha Jet NGEA, the Alpha Jet 2 offers enhanced attack capabilities. A laser ranger is contained in the chisel nose, and a Sagem inertial nav/attack system is fitted.

McDonnell Douglas/BAe Harrier II

Type: Single-seat single-engined attack and reconnaissance fighter with vertical/short takeoff and landing capability used by the US Marine Corps in the close air support role and by the RAF as a Harrier GR.3 replacement.

The Harrier II is a straight development from the earlier Harrier GR.3/AV-8A and is intended to better the earlier model in everything except maximum speed. It remains obviously a Harrier, but with certain external differences: the cockpit, which is closely faired into the fuselage on the Harrier I, has been raised by about 10in (25cm) to give a better view forward, down and to the rear; the wing is greater in area and of increased span, with a consequent improvement in both wing and span loading, and is of a different, supercritical section — one consequence of which is that it can carry a considerable amount of extra fuel — with large, positive circulation flaps to the trailing edge; the outriggers have been

Dimensions	Harrier II
Length (ft/m)	46.33/14.12
Span (ft/m)	30.33/9.24
Height (ft/m)	11.65/3.55
Wing area (sq ft/m²)	230/21.37
Aspect ratio	4.00

Weights	
Empty (lb/kg)	12,922/5,861
Clean takeoff (lb/kg)	20,386/9,247
Max takeoff (lb/kg)	29,750/13,495
Max external load (lb/kg)	9,200/4,173
Hardpoints	7

Power	1 x Pegasus Mk 105/F402-RR-406 tf
Max (lb st/kN)	N/A
Mil (lb st/kN)	21,700/96.4

Fuel	
Internal (lb/kg)	7,142/3,240
External (lb/kg)	7,800/3,538
Fraction	0.35

Loadings	
Max thrust	N/A
Mil thrust	1.06 – 0.73
Wing clean to (lb/sq ft/kg/m²)	89/433
Wing max to (lb/sq ft/kg/m²)	129/632

Performance	
Vmax hi	M = 0.93
Vmax lo	M = 0.88
Ceiling (ft/m)	45,000/13,700 +
Initial climb (ft/min/m/sec)	Not released
Takeoff roll (ft/m)	1,000/300
Landing roll (ft/m)	Vertical

First flight	9 Nov 1978

brought inboard; and a leading-edge root extension has been added to give a positive destabilisation effect for added manoeuvreability. This last feature also provides a vortex to clean up the boundary layer airflow. The engine inlets have a more elliptical shape as well as a single row of auxiliary doors, while lift improvements devices (LIDs) have been installed under the fuselage to control the efflux circulation during vertical takeoff and landing.

Changes below the surface have been just as far reaching. Composite materials are used extensively to save weight; the avionics have been substantially improved, though the fit varies between the AV-8B and the GR.5; and a new stability augmenta-tion system has made a tremendous improvement fo flying qualities when in the hover.

Weapons delivery is effected by the Hughes Angle Rate Bombing System (ARBS), which combines an electro-optical sensor and a televisual con-trast tracker in the nose and can be used for a variety of weapons, in-cluding AGM-65 Maverick; auto-release or depressed sight-line attacks are available.

Differences between the AV-8B and the GR.5 are as follows: the GR.5 has better hardening against bird strikes; the nose cone, wing leading edges,

Below: A Harrier GR.5 with six of its eight underwing pylons carrying cluster bomb units.

and intake lips have all been strengthened, and the windshield is 50 per cent thicker; the GR.5 carries two 25mm Aden cannon in streamlined pods under the fuselage whereas the AV-8B has a single five-barrel GAU-12 25mm rotary cannon on one side and an ammunition tank on the other; the AV-8B has a Stencel ejection seat while the GR.5 has a Martin-Baker Mk 10; and the GR.5 has a moving map display as fitted in the GR.3 while the AV-8B carries the ASN-130 INS, although it may also carry a moving map display in the future.

Both the RAF and USMC have started fielding optimised night attack versions of the Harrier II. The USMC version, the Night Attack Harrier II, features a GEC Forward-Looking Infra-Red (FLIR) system, night vision goggle-compatible cockpit lighting and a colour head-up display.

The British Harrier GR.Mk.7 also features a FLIR above the nose, but a miniature Infra-Red Linescan for all-weather reconnaissance was not installed under the nose in the chin bulge provided. The RAF has ordered 94 Harrier IIs: the first 60 were built to the GR.Mk 5 standard and plans are in hand to upgrade them to GR.Mk.7s. 13 T.10 combat-capable two-seater trainers are also being purchased.

Engine problems prevented the deployment of the USMC's first Night Attack Harrier IIs to the Middle East during Operation *Desert Shield*, but some 60 AV-8Bs flew with the 3rd Marine Air Wing's 11th Marine Air Group from King Abdul Aziz Naval Base at Al Jubayl, in Saudi Arabia. They later flew from forward airstrips during the Coalition ground offensive. In Operation *Desert Storm* the Harriers flew close air support and interdiction missions against targets in Kuwait and Southern Iraq. USMC AV-8Bs also made the first ever US V/STOL attacks from amphibious warfare ships when they launched air strikes from the USS *Nassau* on 21 February 1991. In total, 26 Harrier IIs operated from USMC amphibious warfare ships during *Desert Storm*. Five Harriers were shot down during the war, four of them by Iraqi heat-seeking missiles. This has raised fears about the vulnerability of the AV-8B to this type of weapon because of the location of the aircraft's exhausts near

its engine and wing roots. A programme to improve the AV-8B's self-defence capabilities is now under consideration.

The Spanish and Italian Navies both operate AV-8Bs from their light carriers and they have both signed Memoranda of Understanding to upgrade them to Harrier II Plus standard with Hughes APG-65 radars. Over 100 USMC Harrier IIs are to be converted to this standard and 75 new aircraft built if funding can be secured.

Users
Italy, Spain, UK, USA

Right: An AV-8B drops a stick of Mk 82 500lb (227kg) "slicks" in level flight during bomb trials.

Below: The inner two pylons on the AV-8B's wing are stressed for 2,000lb (907kg), while the outer pylon take 620lb (281kg).

Panavia Tornado IDS

Type: Two-seat twin-engined variable-geometry all-weather interdiction/strike aircraft with reconnaissance capability, optimised for the low-level deep penetration blind first-pass attack and also used in the anti-shipping role. Variants include a long-range interceptor, Tornado ADV, and an Electronic Combat/Reconnaissance aircraft for the Luftwaffe. A Wild Weasel version has been proposed.

Designed to a joint requirement by the United Kingdom, West Germany and Italy, Tornado IDS is arguably the most effective tactical strike and interdiction aircraft in service in the world.

Dimensions	Tornado IDS
Length (ft/m)	54.85/16.72
Span (ft/m)	45,58/13.89
Height (ft/m)	19.52/5.95
Wing area (ft²/m²)	323/30.01
Aspect ratio	6.43—2.46

Weights	
Empty (lb/kg)	31,065/14,091
Clean takeoff (lb/kg)	45,000/20,412
Max takeoff (lb/kg)	61,700/27,987
Max external load (lb/kg)	19,800/8,981
Hardpoints	9

Power	2 x RB199 Mk 103 tf
Max (lb st/kN)	15,800/70.2
Mil (lb st/kg)	9,000/40.0

Fuel	
Internal (lb/kg)	11,250/5,100
External (lb/kg)	14,391/6,530
Fraction	0.25

Loadings	
Max thrust	0.70—0.51
Mil thrust	0.40—0.29
Wing clean to (lb/ft²/kg/m²)	139/680
Wing max to (lb/ft²/kg/m²)	191/933

Performance	
Vmax hi	M = 2.2
Vmax lo	M = 1.2
Ceiling (ft/m)	50,000/15,250
Initial climb (ft/min/m/sec)	40,000/203
Takeoff roll (ft/m)	2,500/760
Landing roll (ft/m)	1,600/500

First flight	14 Aug 1974

The variable-geometry Tornado IDS first entered frontline service in the early 1980s, with production tailing off by the end of the decade. Numerically, the largest user is the Royal Air Force (RAF), which took delivery of some 229 Tornado GR.1/GR.1A. Then comes the German Luftwaffe with 223 Tornado IDS/ECR and the Marineflieger with 109 Tornado IDS/Recce. The Italian Air Force fields a similar number of Tornado IDS. To date, the only other user of the Tornado IDS is the Royal Saudi Air Force (RSAF) which bought 48 under the *Al Yamamah I* deal in 1985. Turkey, Oman, South Korea, Malaysia, Thailand and even Japan have all expressed interest in purchasing the Tornado IDS, but as yet none of these enquiries has been translated into real

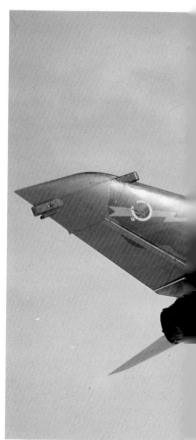

deliveries, although provisional orders have been placed but then cancelled.

Its primary mission is to penetrate deep behind enemy lines, at very low level, to hit targets with a wide variety of ordnance, including general-purpose bombs, cluster bombs, MW-1 or JP.233 dispenser units, laser-guided bombs or air-to-surface missiles and free-fall nuclear bombs. The Texas Instruments ground-mapping radar/terrain-following radar is central to the Tornado IDS's extremely impressive all-weather/night attack capability.

Elements of almost every RAF Tornado GR.1 squadron deployed to the Middle East as part of Operation *Granby* (as the British involvement in the Gulf Crisis was codenamed). By January 1991 three detachments, each with around 15 aircraft, had been established. At Murharraq, on Bahrain, 15 Squadron was the lead

unit supported by elements of 9, 17, 27, 31 and 617 Squadrons. In Saudi Arabia, 31 Squadron was the lead unit at Dhahran, with elements of 9, 14 and 17 Squadrons, while at Tabuk, 16 Squadron was the lead unit, with elements of 2, 9, 14 and 20 Squadrons. Six specialist reconnaissance Tornado GR.1As from 2 and 13 Squadrons were deployed to Dhahran in January. On 6 February 1991, a five aircraft-strong flight was established at Tabuk to use Thermal Imaging Airborne Laser Designator (TIALD) systems. It drew on crews from 2, 13, 14, 16 and 617 Squadrons. The Italian Air Force

Below: An Italian Tornado IDS of 155° Gruppo/36° Stormo toting a pair of Kormoran anti-ship missiles. This weapon is also the principle ordnance carried by Marineflieger Tornados for maritime strike missions.

Above: A pair of Royal Saudi Air Force Tornado IDS's low over the deserts of Saudi Arabia. A robust combatant, the Tornado can carry over 19,840lb (9,000kg) of ordnance, primarily for the deep-strike interdiction mission.

sent eight Tornado IDS' from Gruppi 154, 155 and 156 to Al Dhafra, in Abu Dhabi, in October 1990 as part of Operation *Locust*. A further two aircraft later reinforced the detachment. RSAF Tornados of 7 Squadron and the newly-formed 66 Squadron operated from their home base of Dhahran for the duration of Operation *Desert Storm*.

RAF Tornado GR.1s were heavily involved in all phases of the air offensive against Iraq, flying some 1,600 bombing sorties. During the first three days of the war they delivered more than 100 JP.233 anti-runway munitions. Thereafter, the RAF switched to high level bomb runs with general-purpose bombs. This was considered to be rather ineffective until laser designator systems arrived in the shape of Pave Spike-equipped Buccaneers and Tornado TIALD pods. Tornados from 20 Squadron specialised in using the ALARM anti-radar missile in a Wild Weasel role. By the end of the conflict the RAF Tornado force had dropped around 4,250 free-fall bombs, 950 laser-guided bombs and fired 31 ALARMs.

Controversy still surrounds the casualties suffered by the Tornado. During the conflict, Press pundits claimed the casualties were due to dangerous low-level attacks on runways using JP.233s. Later analysis reveals a diversity of reasons for the losses. The first Tornado lost was carrying general-purpose bombs; the second Tornado casualty was carrying JP233s, but it was hit after it had carried out its attack run. Tornado loss number three was the result of a missile-hit during a lofting bomb run. The fourth Tornado was also lost in a high-lofting bomb run and the fifth was lost when one of its bombs prematurely exploded. A sixth RAF Tornado was shot down during a high-level laser-guided bomb mission. The Italian Air Force also lost one Tornado IDS when it carried out an attack with no support — all its accompanying aircraft had failed to refuel properly from a USAF KC-135. The RSAF and RAF both lost a Tornado apiece in non-combat flying accidents during the Gulf conflict.

Users

Germany, Italy, Saudi Arabia, UK

Right: A German Navy Tornado weapons trials aircraft in the process of carrying out a runway attack courtesy of the MW-1 multi-purpose weapon pack on the centreline. Up to five types of submunitions are ejected from a total of 224 transverse apertures.

Below: Contrails steam from the wingtips as a pair of No. 9 Squadron Tornado GR.1s perform a hard opposition break. Crews from this RAF unit were among those deployed to the Gulf in support of Operation *Granby*. RAF Tornados undertook some 1,600 bombing sorties during the Gulf War in 1991.

SEPECAT Jaguar

Type: Single-seat twin-engined all-weather attack and strike aircraft. Variants include a two-seat trainer and a carrier-based version developed but not proceeded with, while the Jaguar is also used by some nations in the air superiority role.

Back in the early 1960s both the Royal Air Force and the Armée de l'Air were considering the adoption of a supersonic trainer. At the same time, something was wanted to replace the

Dimensions	Jaguar S (GR.1)
Length (ft/m)	50.92/15.52
Span (ft/m)	28.50/8.69
Height (ft/m)	16.13/4.91
Wing area (sq ft/m²)	260/24.16
Aspect ratio	3.12

Weights	
Empty (lb/kg)	16,975/7,700
Clean takeoff (lb/kg)	24,778/11,240
Max takeoff (lb/kg)	34,000/15,425
Max external load (lb/kg)	10,500/4,765
Hardpoints	5

Power	2xRB.172 Adour Mk 104 tf
Max (lb st/kN)	8,040/35.7
Mil (lb st/kN)	5,320/23.6

Fuel	
Internal (lb/kg)	7,213/3,270
External (lb/kg)	6,182/2,805
Fraction	0.29

Loadings	
Max thrust	0.65 − 0.47
Mil thrust	0.43 − 0.31
Wing clean to (lb/sq ft/kg/m²)	95/465
Wing max to (lb/sq ft/kg/m²)	131/638

Performance	
Vmax hi	M = 1.6
Vmax lo	M = 1.1
Ceiling (ft/m)	46,000/14,000
Initial climb (ft/min/m/sec)	Not released
Takeoff roll (ft/m)	2,890/880
Landing roll (ft/m)	1,400/425

First flight	8 Sep 1968

Hunter and Mystère in the attack role. To cut a long story short, British Aerospace were teamed with Breguet (later to be taken over by Dassault) to form a company best known by its acronym, SEPECAT, to develop an aircraft based on a French design and powered by engines built multi-nationally under Rolls-Royce leadership. The supersonic trainer was soon forgotten and the Anglo-French team settled down with their respective air forces to develop a light attack aircraft.

Jaguar has rather the look of a collaborative project. It appears to be large, but appearances are deceptive, and a false impression is given by the ratio of length to span and the stalky undercarriage, which makes it stand high off the ground. Twin engines add to the illusion, although the Adours are small and low powered.

The design of the main gear was conditioned by the requirement for rough field capability, to give plenty of clearance of the external stores. The reason for the choice of two small engines is hard to discover; there were plenty of large ones of sufficient thrust to have done the job. Two engines certainly provides an extra measure of safety — if one packs up or suffers battle damage, the survivor should ensure a safe return to base — but it does not double the safety factor; statistically it improves the attrition rate by about 15 per cent, while cynics could say that there is twice as much to go wrong.

The wing is small, with a moderate aspect ratio, and is highly loaded, all of which gives a low gust response. Short field performance is provided by leading edge slats and double slotted trailing edge flaps to increase lift, but more power to blast it off the ground quicker would have been an advantage. The early Jaguars were powered by the Adour Mk 102, which had rather less thrust than the Mk 104 shown in the table; French Jaguar As have retained the original engine, while the British GR.1s have received the uprated model. Jaguar International, the export version, started out with the Mk 104 (804), but many of them have received the Mk 811, which develops 5,520lb (24,5kN) in military thrust and 8,400lb (37.3kN) with full augmentation.

All single-seat Jaguars are fitted with two 30mm cannon internally, Adens for the British aircrat and DEFA for the French, and Jaguar International can carry two Sidewinders on overwing pylons — a most unusual feature. Payload/range falls between that of the roughly contemporary Harrier and the more modern Tornado.

The primary difference between the British and French Jaguars lies in the avionics fit. The French settled for simplicity with a twin-gyro inertial navigational platform, Doppler radar, a laser rangefinder, navigation and weapons delivery computers, and a radar warning receiver. The British avionics fit was very advanced for its time, with a digital/inertial navigation and weapons aiming sub-system (NAVWASS), a laser rangefinder and marked target seeker in a chisel nose, one of the first HUDs to enter service, and a three-gyro inertial platform; a Ferranti RWR was also carried. The weapons aiming system displayed a continuously computed impact point (CCIP, or 'death dot') on the HUD, giving a miss distance of only 50ft (15m) and making it one of the most accurate

strike aircraft of its day. Adverse weather capability was coupled with long range: 290nm (537km) flown entirely at low level on internal fuel, or more than half as far again using a hi-lo-lo-hi profile.

British Jaguar GR.1s from RAF Coltishall were among the first RAF aircraft to arrive in the Middle East during the Gulf Crisis, with 12 Jaguars deploying to Thumrait, in Oman, on 11 August 1990. They subsequently moved to Muharraq, on Bahrain, to be nearer to Kuwait. During Operation *Desert Storm* the Jaguars flew 618 combat missions, including battlefield air interdiction, anti-shipping strikes and reconnaissance. They fired 608 unguided CVR-7 rockets, 9,600 rounds of 30mm ammunition and dropped 750 bombs and 393 cluster bombs.

French Jaguar As operated from Al Ahsa, in Saudi Arabia, and flew some 615 combat missions during Operation *Desert Storm*. The 28 French Jaguars used a wide variety of ordnance including Belouga cluster bombs and 30 AS.30L laser-guided missiles. These achieved an 80 per cent success rate.

No British or French Jaguars were shot down, although one French aircraft was heavily damaged by a SAM-7 heat-seeking missile in the opening hours of the war.

Below: An RAF SEPECAT Jaguar banks away, revealing LGBs, jamming pods and a fuel tank.

Users
Ecuador, France, India, Nigeria, Oman, UK

Below: A flight of four Omani SEPECAT Jaguars cross the coast and head out to sea. A very robust all-weather attack aircraft, the Jaguar has seen combat action on several different fronts including the Gulf, the Middle East and North Africa.

SOKO J-22 Orao/CNIAR IAR 93

Type: Single-seat twin-engined attack aircraft with two-seat combat-capable training version.

The Orao/IAR-93 is a collaborative programme between Yugoslavia (Orao) and Romania (IAR-93), and is remarkable for the extreme lengths to which the partners have gone to avoid upstaging each other; both the initial prototypes, one made in each country, and the initial two-seat versions first flew on the same day.

Orao/IAR-93 was first produced in an A variant, powered by two Rolls-Royce Viper turbojets, reliable engines that had been used in Yugoslavia for many years. Little has been released about the avionics fit, but this is believed to consist of little more than communications and adverse-weather flight instrumentation.

The type's primary mission is close air support, with low and medium air superiority and point defence an added capability. The thirsty turbojets and fairly modest fuel fraction do not

Dimensions	OraoIAR-93B
Length (ft/m)	45.93/14.00
Span (ft/m)	31.56/9.62
Height (ft/m)	14.60/4.45
Wing area (sq ft/m²)	280/26.00
Aspect ratio	3.56

Weights	
Empty (lb/kg)	12,566/5,700
Clean takeoff (lb/kg)	17,500/7,938
Max takeoff (lb/kg)	23,150/10,500
Max external load (lb/kg)	6,173/2,800
Hardpoints	5

Power	2 x RR Viper 633 tj
Max (lb st/kN)	5,000/22.2
Mil (lb st/kN)	4,200/18.9

Fuel	
Internal (lb/kg)	4,465/2,025
External (lb/kg)	2,787/1,264
Fraction	0.26

Loadings	
Max thrust	0.57 − 0.43
Mil thrust	0.46 − 0.35
Wing clean to (lb/sq ft/kg/m²)	63/305
Wing max to (lb/sq ft/kg/m²)	83/404

Performance	
Vmax hi	M = 0.92
Vmax lo	M = 0.95
Ceiling (ft/m)	42,600/13,000
Initial climb (ft/min/m/sec)	12,992/66
Takeoff roll (ft/m)	2,260/690
Landing roll (ft/m)	3,450/1,050

First flight	21 Oct 1974

give a wide a radius of action, but in the CAS mission this is not too important. Two 23mm GSh-23 twin barrel cannon are fitted internally for straffing or air-to-air use, with a capacity of 200 rounds per gun.

The B variant, which first flew towards the end of 1983, has afterburners fitted to its Viper 663 engines, which has improved short takeoff performance and almost doubled the initial rate of climb.

The Romanian Air Force has some 35 Oraos in service with a further 165 on order, while the Yugoslav Federal Air Force has just over 100 for attack, reconnaissance and training. The latter were in action over Slovenia and Croatia after civil war broke out in the summer of 1991. American-made AGM-65 Maverick air-to-ground missiles and British BL-755 cluster bombs have been delivered by the Yugoslav Oraos.

Users
Romania, Yugoslavia

Below: The light attack field is one in which many countries have experimented, and the SOKO Orao, seen here armed with a rocket pod, is no more than an average product.

Bottom: The Orao/IAR-93 design was conditioned by the engines available, in this case Rolls-Royce Vipers. Even with reheat it is firmly subsonic.

Mitsubishi F-1

Type: Single-seat twin-engined attack aircraft with limited counter-air capability, developed from a two-seat supersonic trainer derivative of the SEPECAT Jaguar.

The Mitsubishi F-1 stemmed from a requirement for a supersonic trainer intended to provide the transition from subsonic training aircraft to the supersonic F-104 Starfighters and F-4 Phantoms of the Japanese Air Self Defence Force. It was probably also intended to give the Japanese experience in the design of supersonic aircraft, and the design was based on that of the SEPECAT

Jaguar, itself once intended as a trainer, to which it bears a distinct family resemblance. Early trials of the trainer having proved successful, it was decided to develop it into a single-seat close support aircraft.

The resulting Mitsubishi F-1 looks rather like a Jaguar that has somehow gone wrong. It is longer, but has a smaller span and less wing area; the fin has been completely redesigned to be shorter and broader; the stalky gear is gone, replaced by a shorter and more orthodox-looking undercarriage; the dorsal spine has become less angular; and while the front end is reminiscent of the Jaguar

Dimensions	Mitsubishi F-1
Length (ft/m)	58.58/17.85
Span (ft/m)	25.85/7.88
Height (ft/m)	14.69/4.48
Wing area (sq ft/m²)	228/21.19
Aspect ratio	2.93

Weights	
Empty (lb/kg)	14,017/6,360
Clean takeoff (lb/kg)	21,080/9,560
Max takeoff (lb/kg)	30,146/13,675
Max external load (lb/kg)	6,000/2,720
Hardpoints	5

Power	2 x TF40-IHI-801A tf
Max (lb st/kN)	7,305/32.5
Mil (lb st/kN)	5,115/22.7

Fuel	
Internal (lb/kg)	6,565/2,980
External (lb/kg)	4,276/1,940
Fraction	0.31

Loadings	
Max thrust	0.69 – 0.48
Mil thrust	0.49 – 0.34
Wing clean to (lb/sq ft/kg/m²)	92/451
Wing max to (lb/sq ft/kg/m²)	132/646

Performance	
Vmax hi	M = 1.60
Vmax lo	M = 0.80
Ceiling (ft/m)	50,000/15,250
Initial climb (ft/min/m/sec)	19,680/100
Takeoff roll (ft/m)	4,200/1,280
Landing roll (ft/m)	N/A

First flight	1977

T-2 trainer the rear cockpit is faired into provide an avionics bay. Despite the increase in length, empty weight has been reduced by nearly 3,000lb (1,360kg). The Adour turbofans have been retained, built under licence in Japan by Ishikawajima-Harima, but the 30mm cannon are replaced by the rapid-firing M61A Vulcan six-barrel 20mm Gun with 750 rounds, mounted low on the left side.

The Japanese Self Defence Forces are committed to eschew offensive action in any shape or form, which makes the attack role rather invidious, and the F-1 is known to the Japanese as a support fighter, a cosmetic description if ever there was one. In practice it is assigned to the attack of any seaborne invasion force, carrying the indigenous ASM-1 anti-ship missile, a launch-and-leave weapon; alternative loads are iron bombs or unguided rocket pods. Typical radius of action with two ASM-1s and a single 186.6Imp gal (830lit) drop tank is 295nm (550km) using a hi-lo-lo-hi mission profile, reducing to about 200nm (370km) for the lo-lo mission. Two Sidewinders are normally carried on wingtip rails for self-defence.

The cockpit is cramped by American standards but well suited to the Japanese physique, and handling is reported to be 'docile'. If the F-1 has a fault it lies in the avionics, which are fairly basic.

In April 1986 it was announced that the F-1 is to receive a service life extension from 3,500 to 4,500 hours, equivalent to about another three years flying time; an autopilot is to be installed, launchers for AIM-9L are to be added, and a stronger windshield, designed to stop a medium sized bird at 500kt (926km/h), will be fitted.

Some 77 F-1s were produced for the JASDF from 1978 onwards and 94 T-2 two-seat trainer aircraft were built up to 1988. Five T-2s serve in the JASDF's "aggressor" squadron based at Tsuiki and other T-2s are used for advanced fast-jet training. They also are flown by the *Blue Impulse* aerobatic team.

User
Japan

Left: The faired-in rear crew position reduces the F-1 pilot's rear view to nil.

Below: The Mitsubishi F-1 is officially a support fighter for Japan's Air Self-Defence Force.

Mikoyan MiG-27 Flogger

Type: Single-seat single-engined development of the MiG-23 multi-role fighter adapted for the tactical strike and close air support roles.

The MiG-23 Flogger counter-air fighter could reasonably be described as the first Soviet attempt to produce a tactical aircraft with a useful payload/range. As a fighter it was uninspired, and in both avionics and performance it fell short of the American Phantom, the aircraft that

Dimensions	MiG-27 Flogger-J
Length (ft/m)	54.00/16.46
Span (ft/m)	46.75/14.25 max
Height (ft/m)	14.33/4.37
Wing area (sq ft/m²)	325/30.20
Aspect ratio	6.27 – 2.27

Weights	
Empty (lb/kg)	24,250/11,000
Clean takeoff (lb/kg)	34,764/15,770
Max takeoff (lb/kg)	44,312/20,100
Max external load (lb/kg)	8,820/4,000
Hardpoints	5

Power	
	1 x R29B tj
Max (lb st/kN)	25,350/112.7
Mil (lb st/kN)	17,635/78.4

Fuel	
Internal (lb/kg)	9,914/4,500
External (lb/kg)	4,100/1,860
Fraction	0.29

Loadings	
Max thrust	0.73 – 0.57
Mil thrust	0.51 – 0.40
Wing clean to (lb/sq ft/kg/m²)	107/522
Wing max to (lb/sq ft/kg/m²)	136/666

Performance	
Vmax hi	M = 1.6
Vmax lo	M = 0.95
Ceiling (ft/m)	46,000/14,000
Initial climb (ft/min/m/sec)	N/A
Takeoff roll (ft/m)	2,950/900
Landing roll (ft/m)	2,950/900

First flight	c.1970

it was intended to match. A single-seater, it offered an abysmal view out of the cockpit, with little rear visibility and the forward view obstructed by heavy front screen and canopy framing, though Soviet pilots have commented that this is something that they have got used to and can live with.

Flogger does, however, have certain virtues: it is strong, easy to produce, which means that it can be built cheaply and in large numbers, and it has variable-sweep wings which can be manually set to angles of 16°, 45° or 72°. Minimum sweep reduces takeoff and landing speeds, with a consequent reduction in the runway distance required, increases range and endurance, and permits heavier loads to be carried; intermediate sweep gives optimum turning performance; and maximum sweep reduces drag for acceleration and in high-speed flight, while at high speed and low level it reduces gust response and gives a smooth ride. Coupled with a decent fuel fraction and radius of action, Flogger's aerodynamic versatility made it an obvious choice for the attack role.

The first attack variant was the MiG-23BN, essentially the fighter version with a redesigned front fuselage, rather shorter than the original, which vaguely resembled that of the Jaguar and was quickly dubbed 'utkonos', or 'duck-nose' by the Soviet pilots, The cockpit was revised to give a better view downwards throughout the front quarter, and was armoured against ground fire, while the new nose, freed from the necessity of carrying a large air-to-air radar, sloped sharply down and contained a laser rangefinder.

The MiG-23BN was no more than an interim measure, and an extensive redesign resulted in the MiG-27. The Mach 2 capability of the original fighter, which had been retained in the MiG-23BN, was acknowledged to have no operational value at the low levels where attack missions are carried out, and was deleted: fixed engine inlets were adopted instead of the variable ones used previously, along with a shorter and simpler engine nozzle. These changes limited top speed to Mach 1.6, which for operational purposes is still unusable, and produced a considerable saving in weight, which in turn allowed the payload to be increased. The gear was beefed up to cope with the higher maximum weights, and larger wheels and tyres added, which needed bulged doors to accommodate them; it has been speculated that this was also to give the MiG-27 a measure of rough field performance.

For the first time hardpoints were added to the movable portions of the wings: these carry drop tanks only, and do not swivel. The tanks can be carried for the early part of the mission then jettisoned when anything other than minimum wing sweep is required. The avionics are more comprehensive than those of the MiG-23BN, and include a Doppler radar, a radio altimeter and a terrain-avoidance radar mounted in the nose. A laser ranger/marked target seeker is also carried, along with what is believed to be air-to-ground missile guidance radar.

The final major change has been the adoption of a 23mm six barrel Gatling-type cannon carried internally on the centreline, replacing the GSh-23 carried by the fighter.

The first version of the MiG-27 (Flogger-D) entered frontline service in 1974 and production of the three main versions continued until 1984.

Right: Plain inlets, mudguards and the laser ranger can be seen on this view of a MiG-27.

Below: A MiG-23BM Flogger-F hybrid fighter-bomber.

The MiG-23BM (Flogger-F) was a hybrid fighter-bomber and featured much of the equipment used on the MiG-23. The definitive attack version was the MiG-27M (Flogger-J), which was identified in 1981 and boasted a laser rangefinder and laser designator for use with laser-guided bombs.

Production started in 1984 of the Indian version, the HAL-built Bahadur, which is a copy of the MiG-27M built under licence. A specialist naval version was also produced and tested on the Soviet carrier *Tbilisi* during the late 1980s.

More than 8,818lb (4000kg) of ordnance can be carried, including AS-7 "Kerry" radio command-guided missiles, AS-14 "Kedge" electro-optical guided bombs, TN-1200 tactical nuclear bombs, FAB-500-bombs, cluster bombs, BETAB retard bombs and AA-8 "Aphid" high-explosive air-to-air heat-seeking missiles.

Users:
India, Soviet Union

Sukhoi Su-17/-20/-22 Fitter

Type: Single-seat single-engined variable-geometry attack fighter with some counter-air capability. Variants include two-seat trainers and a pod can be carried for reconnaissance missions.

While the Soviet MiG Design Bureau has long been known for its sleek jet fighters, the Sukhoi Design Bureau has generally concentrated on building tough ground attack aircraft over the years.

The Sukhoi Su-17/-20/-22 family (NATO codename Fitter) is the archi-typical Sukhoi product, in service with some 16 air forces around the world. Sukhoi's aircraft first took to the air in the early 1950s as a fixed-wing strike fighter, designated the Su-7 (Fitter-A). In the late 1960s the design was significantly upgraded by the provision of a new engine (the AL-7F) and variable-geometry wings. These improvements doubled the warload, halved the take-off distance and

	Su-17 Fitter-H	Su-22 Fitter-J
Dimensions		
Length (ft/m)	51.83/15.80	51.83/15.80
Span (ft/m)	45.92/14.00 max	45.92/14.00 max
Height (ft/m)	15.58/4.75	15.58/4.75
Wing area (sq ft/m²)	432/40.10	432/40.10
Aspect ratio	4.89 − 2.49	4.89 − 2.49
Weights		
Empty (lb/kg)	22,500/10,206	21,715/9,850
Clean takeoff (lb/kg)	34,170/15,500	33,115/15,020
Max takeoff (lb/kg)	42,330/19,200	43,900/19,900
Max external load (lb/kg)	8,160/3,700	10,785/4,890
Hardpoints	8	8
Power		
	1 x AL-21F	1 x R-29B
Max (lb st/kN)	24,700/109.8	25,350/112.7
Mil (lb st/kN)	17,200/76.4	17,635/78.4
Fuel		
Internal (lb/kg)	10,765/4,885	10,765/4,885
External (lb/kg)	5,495/2,490	5,495/2,490
Fraction	0.32	0.33
Loadings		
Max thrust	0.72 − 0.58	0.77 − 0.58
Mil thrust	0.50 − 0.41	0.53 − 0.40
Wing clean to (lb/sq ft/kg/m²)	79/387	77/375
Wing max to (lb/sq ft/kg/m²)	98/479	102/496
Performance		
Vmax hi	M = 2.09	M = 2.09
Vmax lo	M = 1.06	M = 1.06
Ceiling (ft/m)	Not released	Not released
Initial climb (ft/min/m/sec)	44,290/225	44,290/225
Takeoff roll (ft/m)	"Moderate"	"Moderate"
Landing roll (ft/m)	"Moderate"	"Moderate"
First flight	2 Aug 1966 (prototype)	N/A

increased operational range by some 30 per cent.

Since 1970, when the Su-17 entered service with Soviet Frontal Aviation, eight main versions have been produced. The Su-17/-20 (Fitter-C) were the main pre-production and production versions, with AL-7F-1 and AL-21F-3 engines respectively. The Su-20M (Fitter-D) had a terrain avoidance radar and laser rangefinder fitted to the nose. Su-20Us were the two-seat trainers. Tumanski R-29Bs were fitted to the Su-22 (Fitter-F) and Su-22UM (Fitter-G) two-seat trainer. Improved weapons capability was the main refinement on the Su-22M-1 and M-3 (Fitter-H). The Su-22M-2 (Fitter-J) is the export version of the Su-22M-1. The final version is the Su-22M-4 (Fitter-K) which is powered by an improved Lyuka AL-21F-3 engine. It is the definitive version of the Sukhoi fighter and can carry conventional bombs, rockets, chemical bombs, nuclear weapons, laser-guided bombs and anti-ship missiles. A full electronic countermeasures and chaff/flare dispensing suite is fitted.

Su-7s saw action with the Egyptian and Syrian Air Forces during the Yom Kippur War of 1973, and later models have also seen plenty of action. Two Libyan Su-22M-2s were shot down by US Navy Tomcats in the 1981 Gulf of Sirte air battle. Soviet and Afghan Sukhois were heavily engaged throughout the Afghan War, in their intended air-to-ground role.

The largest user is Soviet Frontal Aviation which boasts some 800 examples of various models. The Soviet Navy also uses the Sukhoi in the anti-shipping role. Poland, Czechoslovakia, Bulgaria and Afghanistan all use the Su-22M-4. The German Luftwaffe is the latest recipient after it took over control of the old East German Air Force. Poland and Hungary are reported to be interested in buying these now-redundant aircraft.

Users
Afghanistan, Algeria, Angola, Bulgaria, Czechoslovakia, Egypt, Hungary, Iraq, Libya, Peru, Poland, Soviet Union, Syria, Vietnam, Yemen.

Below: An Su-17M-4 Fitter-K looses off an AS-7 "Kerry".

77

Sukhoi Su-24 Fencer

Type: Two-seat twin-engined long-range strike and interdiction aircraft with some reconnaissance capability.

Work began on the Sukhoi Su-24 (NATO code-name Fencer) in the mid-1960s, and the aircraft entered service from 1974 onwards. The 900 examples in service with the Soviet Frontal Aviation are optimised for deep strike/interdiction missions with both conventional and nuclear air-to-ground weapons.

There are at least eight versions of the Su-24. The Sukhoi T.6-1 was the first prototype, which was a fixed-wing aircraft. The initial production variant was called Fencer-A by NATO and the latest production version is known as the Fencer-E. Fencer-As featured a reshaped radome; Fencer-Cs had radar warning receivers fitted to the fuselage and tail. Su-24MKs (Fencer-D) had a new radome for fully-automated terrain-following radar, wing fences, in-flight refuelling and a different fin shape. The Fencer-D (Mod) is the export version of the Su-24MK. A specialist reconnaissance version is the Su-24MR (Fencer-E) and the Su-24MP (Fencer-F) is a dedicated electronic warfare platform.

The Su-24MK is considered the

Dimensions	Su-24 Fencer
Length (ft/m)	73.40/22.4
Span (ft/m)	62/18.9
Height (ft/m)	20.6/6.3
Wing area (ft²/m²)	452/42.00
Aspect ratio	7.06—2.52

Weights	
Empty (lb/kg)	41,890/19,000
Clean takeoff (lb/kg)	64,000/29,000
Max takeoff (lb/kg)	87,080/39,500
Max external load (lb/kg)	24,250/11,000
Hardpoints	9

Power	2 x AL-21F3 tj
Max (lb st/kN)	24,692/11,200
Mil (lb st/kg)	17,196/7,800

Fuel	
Internal (lb/kg)	22,928/10,400
External (lb/kg)	18,750/8,500
Fraction	0.34

Loadings	
Max thrust	0.76—0.56
Mil thrust	0.53—0.39
Wing clean to (lb/ft²/kg/m²)	142/691
Wing max to (lb/ft²/kg/m²)	193/941

Performance	
Vmax hi	M = 2.18
Vmax lo	M = 1.20
Ceiling (ft/m)	57,400/17,500
Initial climb (ft/min/m/sec)	28,000/142
Takeoff roll (ft/m)	Short
Landing roll (ft/m)	Short

First flight	1970

definitive version and is in widespread service with Soviet Frontal Aviation. A wide range of air-to-ground ordnance can be carried, including AS-7 Kerry radio command-guided bombs, AS-9 Kyle anti-radiation missiles, AS-10 Karen electro-optical guided missiles, AS-12 Kegler anti-radiation missiles and AS-14 Kedge semi-active laser-guided missiles. Freefall nuclear bombs and stand-off nuclear missiles, such as the AS-11 Kilter or AS-16 Kickback can also be carried, as can freefall conventional bombs and external drop tanks. Stores are carried on five fuselage hardpoints and four wing hardpoints, the latter swivelling to accommodate wing changes.

At the height of the Cold War in the early 1980s, two regiments were forward-based in East Germany to threaten NATO supply bases in Britain, but they have now been withdrawn back to the Soviet Union. Export customers to date include Libya, which has received 15 examples; Syria has received its first batch of 15 and Iraq received at least 24 before the Gulf War.

Users:
Iran, Iraq, Libya, Soviet Union, Syria

Bottom: The Su-24 Fencer-C two-seater attack aircraft first entered service in 1981.

Below: The similarity of the Su-24 to the F-111 can be seen to good effect in this view.

Sukhoi Su-25 Frogfoot

Type: Single-seat twin-engined close air support aircraft. Two-seat trainer, the Su-25UB, is also in service and has carried out deck-landing trials on Soviet Navy aircraft carriers.

The Sukhoi Su-25 (NATO code-name Frogfoot) began life in the mid-1970s as the first Soviet purpose-built close air support aircraft since the Second World War. The Su-25's development subsequently mirrors the experience of Soviet Frontal Aviation units in Afghanistan.

In many ways the Su-25 Frogfoot is an enigma to the West. In some ways it appears to be the Soviet equivalent of the Fairchild A-10A, while bearing a vague resemblance to the losing competitor in the A-X programme, the Northrop A-9A. The dimensions are known only approximately; and the weights are very much a matter of guesswork, with no two sources seeming to guess the same. All that can be said with any certainty is that the Frogfoot is smaller, lighter and faster than the A-10A. The American DoD credits it with an operational radius of about 300nm (556km), presumably with a standard warload, which is probably about half the maximum; the mission profile is not given, but can be assumed to be at medium to low level. That is considerably less than the A-10 can achieve, although radius of action is basically irrelevant for both types, loiter time being more important, while penetration of more than a few miles into defended airspace is all but suicidal.

An experimental unit, the 200th Independent Guards Aviation Squadron, was deployed to Shindand Air Base in January 1982 and a forward operating base set up at Bagram Air Base. The aircraft was used extensively over the next seven years and by the time the Soviets finally withdrew in 1989, some 50 Su-25s were deployed in Afghanistan. A wide range of ordnance was used in battle, including RBK-250 cluster bombs, cannons and BETAB retard bombs. AS-7 "Kerry" air-to-surface missiles were also used against Mujhadeen guerillas hiding in caves. Iraqi Air Force Su-25s have also seen action against Kurdish guerrillas and two were shot down by US F-15s during the Gulf War.

While often being compared with the US A-10A Thunderbolt II, the Su-25 differs greatly because it is not as heavily armoured as the American "tankbuster". The experience in Afghanistan has led to self-defence systems such as chaff/flare dispensers being fitted as standard operational equipment.

Versions of the Frogfoot in service include the Su-25UB (Frogfoot-B) two-two-seat operational conversion and

Dimensions	Su-25 Frogfoot
Length (ft/m)	49.22/15.00
Span (ft/m)	46.90/14.30
Height (ft/m)	16.41/5.00
Wing area (ft²/m²)	420/39.00
Aspect ratio	5.24

Weights	
Empty (lb/kg)	19,200/8,709
Clean takeoff (lb/kg)	28,000/12,700
Max takeoff (lb/kg)	40,000/18,144
Max external load (lb/kg)	12,000/5,443
Hardpoints	10

Power	2 x R13-300 tj
Max (lb st/kN)	N/A
Mil (lb st/kN)	11,250/50.0

Fuel	
Internal (lb/kg)	8,400/3,810
External (lb/kg)	2,060/934
Fraction	0.30

Loadings	
Max thrust	N/A
Mil thrust	0.80—0.56
Wing clean to (lb/ft²/kg/m²)	67/327
Wing max to (lb/ft²/kg/m²)	95/464

Performance	
Vmax hi	N/A
Vmax lo	M = 0.74
Ceiling (ft/m)	N/A
Initial climb (ft/min/m/sec)	N/A
Takeoff roll (ft/m)	1,500/457
Landing roll (ft/m)	1,200/366

First flight	1977

weapons training model, which made a carrier-deck landing on the *Tbilisi* during 1989 courtesy of an arrestor hook. The latest version is the Su-25T, which features improved fuel capacity, avionics, armour and attack systems. The export version of this model is designated the Su-25TK.

Foreign users include the Czech Air Force, which was the first export customer in 1985, and the Hungarian and Afghan Air Forces. Iraq recieved 30 Su-25s in the mid-1980s. In 1991 the Soviet Air Forces in Germany boasted some 85 Su-25s, spread between three fighter bomber wings, indicating that Frontal Aviation regards it as a potent weapon in conventional warfare, not just counter-insurgency operations.

The Su-25s are produced at a factory in Tbilisi in the Republic of Georgia which is trying to secede from the old Soviet Union. This places a big question mark over the future production of this robust aircraft.

Users
Czechoslovakia, Hungary, Iraq, Soviet Union

Above: Often assumed to be a mirror image of the A-10, the Frogfoot resembles the A-9.

Below: The four main pylons under each wing are the principal warload carriers.

Saab AJ 37 Viggen

Type: Single-seat single-engined attack fighter optimised for deployed basing, with some adverse weather capability. The AJ 37 is one of a family of four types; the other aircraft are fighter, reconnaissance and two-seat trainer versions.

Sweden has a small population relative to the area of the country and

Dimensions	AJ 37 Viggen
Length (ft/m)	53.48/16.30
Span (ft/m)	34.77/10.60
Height (ft/m)	18.00/5.49
Wing area (sq ft/m²)	495/46.00
Aspect ratio	2.44

Weights	
Empty (lb/kg)	23,150/10,500 (est)
Clean takeoff (lb/kg)	34,450/15,625 (est)
Max takeoff (lb/kg)	40,000/18,145 (est)
Max external load (lb/kg)	13,200/6,000
Hardpoints	7

Power	1 x RM.8A tf
Max (lb st/kN)	25,990/115.5
Mil (lb st/kN)	14,750/65.6

Fuel	
Internal (lb/kg)	9,750/4,423
External (lb/kg)	(est)N/A
Fraction	0.28

Loadings	
Max thrust	0.75 − 0.65
Mil thrust	0.43 − 0.37
Wing clean to (lb/sq ft/kg/m²)	70/340
Wing max to (lb/sq ft/kg/m²)	81/394

Performance	
Vmax hi	M = 2 +
Vmax lo	M = 1.1
Ceiling (ft/m)	55,000/16,750
Initial climb (ft/min/m/sec)	40,000/203
Takeoff roll (ft/m)	1,312/400
Landing roll (ft/m)	1,640/500

First flight	8 Feb 1967 (prototype)

the length of border that it must defend, and its political stance is determinedly neutral. Nowhere is Swedish neutrality more marked than in its determination to remain self-sufficient in the field of combat aircraft. Since 1945 this policy has resulted in a remarkable string of home-brew fast jets, of which the Viggen is the most recent to enter service. Also notable is the Swedish tendency to ignore what other countries are producing and predicting, a tendency that has turned out two aircraft which resemble nothing else flying. The 1950s-vintage Draken could only be described as futuristic, while its successor, the mid-1960s Viggen, can equally be described as unique. But then, the missions that Swedish fighters are called on to fly have no exact equivalent in the Western world.

The design of multi-role fighters inevitably involves compromise. Attack, interception, reconnaissance and air superiority all have different priorities, and optimisation for any one will normally degrade others. This was overcome with the Viggen by producing four different variants — five if the two reconnaissance missions are counted — using a common airframe. The other aspect common to all is the ability to deploy away from fixed airfields, which in time of war would be targeted in advance. This dispersed basing would be very difficult to knock out; for the most part it consists of straight stretches of road, widened and strenthened and provided with command, communication and repair facilities.

To make the most of the dispersed bases, and to enable it to operate from damaged airfields, the Viggen was designed with a remarkable short field capability and can take off in 1,312ft (400m) and land back in 1,640ft (500m). The takeoff distance is not startling by modern standards — it can be equalled by many other types — but where they need at least three times the distance to land back, meaning in practice that while they could take off from a damaged field they could not return to it, the Viggen's landing run is barely more than its takeoff roll. Three factors account for this: a hard, no-flare carrier-style landing with a sink rate rather more than most land-based fighters could accommodate; a precision landing approach system which allows a precision touchdown; and reverse thrust from the engines for braking. Taking into account Sweden's icy conditions in winter, reverse thrust is essential, as any attempt at orthodox braking would be sporty to say the least.

The Viggen was the first fast jet to enter service with a canard configuration. This was adopted to overcome the worst faults of the delta wing; the canards are fixed, with a trailing edge control surface, and while similar in appearance to those on Rafale and EAP they are in fact quite different, those on the latter being all-moving surfaces. As used on the Viggen, the canard foreplanes simply give good STOL performance to a delta-wing layout, adding lift and enhancing wing lift, the delta being adopted for its supersonic flight characteristics.

The Viggen was really a little ahead of its time: a few years later, it might have benefited from relaxed stability and fly-by-wire, which could greatly have improved its manoeuvring qualities. A few years after it entered Swedish Service it was evaluated for NATO against the Mirage F.1E and the F-16 Fighting Falcon, and while the Swedish aircraft had better short field performance than the F-16, the eventual winner, it lost out badly in other areas. In the attack mission, carrying six 500lb (227kg) bombs, its low-level radius of action was 257nm (476km) compared to the 295nm (547km) of the F-16, reflecting a lower fuel fraction and a more thirsty engine. Manoeuvre capability with the same load was much worse: at Mach 0.7 at sea level the F-16 had a turn radius of about 4,500ft (1,372m) against the Viggen's 11,000ft (3,353m).

The last production Viggen was delivered to the Swedish Air Force in June 1990 after more than 300 had been produced, including 137 JA 37 interceptors, 82 AJ 37 attack aircraft, 47 SF/SH 37 maritime attack/reconnaissance aircraft and 18 SK 37s.

User
Sweden

Right: The Viggen was designed to cope with both dispersed basing and the icy conditions found in Sweden.

Below: With a total of seven hardpoints (four underwing; three underfuselage), the AJ 37 Viggen can pack quite a punch in the attack role. A quartet of rocket pods can be seen on this AJ 37, one of 82 for the Swedish Air Force.

Saab JAS 39 Gripen

Type: Single-seat multi-role combat aircraft.

The Swedish Air Force expects to take delivery of its first Gripens in 1993. The new multi-role fighter is to replace the Swedish Air Force's ageing Drakens and Viggens in air defence, strike, close air support, reconnaissance and anti-shipping missions.

Work began in the early 1980s and the first Gripen took to the skies on its maiden flight in 1988. Eventually it is hoped to equip some 21 to 23 squadrons, with initial orders running to 140 aircraft and possible production running to 350 airframes.

The Gripen follows in the great tradition of Swedish combat aircraft and features a delta wing and canard foreplanes. A fly-by-wire control system and moveable canard foreplanes indicate that the Gripen is a highly-advanced combat aircraft in roughly the same class as the F-16 and Tornado.

Like all Swedish aircraft, the Gripen is optimised for operations from dispersed sites. Its small size compared to the Viggen means it is much easier to hide.

To cut costs the Swedes tried to embark on a collaborative venture, but this fell through when potential partners insisted on a two-engined aircraft. Cost savings were achieved by Volvo Flygmotor adapting the General Electric F404-400 turbofan engine, the purchase of the flight control system from Lear Seiger, the auxilliary power unit from Microturbo, the inertial navigation system from Honeywell and the prototype wings from British Aerospace.

The development of the Gripen has not been without problems. A year's delay was caused by the crash of the prototype due to flight control system software problems. After extensive re-writing the software was judged safe and the second prototype made its first flight in 1990.

With the project now at such an advanced stage it seems highly unlikely that the Swedish Air Force will pull out, although defence cuts may force a reduced production run. Export prospects though, look good, with Finland already expressing an interest. Newly-liberated countries in Eastern and Central Europe could also be likely Gripen customers.

Dimensions	JAS 39 Gripen
Length (ft/m)	46.3/14.00
Span (ft/m)	26.3/8.00
Height (ft/m)	15.5/4.70
Wheel track	8.7/2.60
Wheelbase	17.5/5.30

Weights	
Max takeoff (lb/kg)	17,635/8,000
Hardpoints	7

Power	1 x RM12 tf
Max (lb st/kN)	18,100/80.5
Mil (lb st/kN)	12,140/54.0

Performance	
Takeoff roll (ft/m)	2,625/800
Landing roll (ft/m)	2,625/800
Max level speed	supersonic
g limit	+9

First flight	9 December 1988

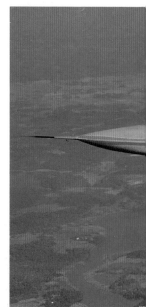

Above: Although only a pair of AIM-9 AAMs are visible, the Gripen can carry other stores on five more weapons stations.

Below: A single-seat fighter and attack aircraft, the Gripen is set to replace the Viggen in Swedish service.

BAe Buccaneer S.Mk 2B

Type: Two-seat twin-engined attack bomber designed specifically for the low level mission.

In spite of being considered by some to be in the vintage aircraft class, 12 RAF Buccaneers played a vital role in the Gulf Conflict. The Buccaneer first went into production in the 1950s as a carrier-borne strike aircraft for the Royal Navy's Fleet Air Arm. With the demise of the British TSR.2 project and the cancellation of orders for American F-111s, the RAF ordered the Buccaneer in 1968 as a low-level strike aircraft. The Buccaneer's long

unrefuelled range — more than 2,000nm (3,706km) — and large warload of four internally-carried 1,000lb (454kg) bombs, made it ideal for deep penetration missions.

The first combat user of the Buccaneer was the South African Air Force (SAAF), who bought six before arms sanctions were imposed on the country in the 1960s. SAAF Buccaneers were in the frontline of the country's undeclared war with SWAPO guerillas, flying numerous strike missions deep into Angola.

In 1990 the British MoD announced that the Buccaneers were to be retired as part of the *Options for*

Dimensions	Buccaneer S.2
Length (ft/m)	63.42/19.33
Span (ft/m)	44.00/13.41
Height (ft/m)	16.25/4.95
Wing area (ft²/m²)	514.7/47.82
Aspect ratio	3.76

Weights	
Empty (lb/kg)	30,000/13,610
Clean takeoff (lb/kg)	46,000/20,865
Max takeoff (lb/kg)	62,000/28,125
Max external load (lb/kg)	12,000/5,440
Hardpoint	4

Power	2 x Spey Mk 101 tf
Max (lb st/kN)	N/A
Mil (lb st/kN)	11,200/49.8

Fuel	
Internal (lb/kg)	15,612/7,080
External (lb/kg)	3,900/1,770
Fraction	0.34

Loadings	
Max thrust	0.49—0.36
Mil thrust	N/A
Wing clean to (lb/ft²/kg/m²)	89/436
Wing max to (lb/ft²/kg/m²)	120/588

Performance	
Vmax hi	M = 0.92
Vmax lo	M = 0.85
Ceiling (ft/m)	40,000/12,200
Initial climb (ft/min/m/sec)	7,000/36
Takeoff roll (ft/m)	long
Landing roll (ft/m)	long

First flight	May 1963

Change process and replaced by maritime strike Tornados. A few months later the Buccaneers were called into action at the height of Operation *Desert Storm*. On 23 January 1991, the two Lossiemouth squadrons, Nos. 12 and 208, were ordered to dispatch the first of 12 aircraft to Muharraq, in Bahrain, to act as laser designators for RAF Tornado GR.1s. Carrying Westinghouse AN/AVQ-23 Pave Spike pods the Buccaneers flew their first mission on 2 February against a road bridge across the Euphrates at As Samawah in Iraq.

By this point of the war the RAF Tornado force had switched totally to precision attack missions with laser-guided bombs against Iraqi bridges, airfields and industrial targets. Without the Buccaneers this would not have been possible because of the lack of TIALD designator pods compatable with Tornado GR.1s. In the last week of the war the Buccaneers started to carry their own laser-guided bombs. During raids they would first designate for Tornados, then swing back over targets to drop their own munitions. In their final attack of the war, on 27 February against Shayka Mayhar air base, two Iraqi An-12 transport aircraft were destroyed by Buccaneers.

User
UK

Below: The Buccaneer remains a potent aircraft despite its rather ungainly appearance.

BAe Hawk

Type: Two-seat single-engined advanced trainer developed for clear-weather air defence, close air support, attack and anti-shipping missions. Hawk 200 is a single seat attack/fighter, and the US Navy has adopted the T-45A Goshawk, navalised by McDonnell Douglas, as its new standard advanced trainer.

The mid-1960s requirement for an advanced trainer for the Royal Air Force was originally to have been met by the SEPECAT Jaguar, but development of this aircraft made it rather more capable than had been specified, and consequently rather more expensive. The UK and France then went separate ways, the latter combining with Germany to produce the Alpha Jet while the British requirement resulted in the Hawk.

As was only to be expected, the Alpha Jet and the Hawk became rivals in the export market, with the French trainer, slightly ahead in timing, threatening to scoop the field with the benefit of Dassault's aggressive marketing. The Hawk is very similar in size and general layout, the main difference being that it has only one engine to the Alpha Jet's two, the resulting increased saftey margin apparently being a strong argument

Dimensions	Hawk T.1	Hawk 60	Hawk 200
Length (ft/m)	38.92/11.86	38.92/11.86	37.33/11.38
Span (ft/m)	30.83/9.40	30.83/9.40	30.83/9.40
Height (ft/m)	13.16/4.00	13.16/4.00	13.67/4.17
Wing area (sq ft/m²)	180/16.69	180/16.69	180/16.69
Aspect ratio	5.28	5.28	5.28
Weights			
Empty (lb/kg)	7,450/3,380	8,015/3,635	8,765/3,975
Clean takeoff (lb/kg)	10,700/4,854	11,350/5,148	12,100/5,490
Max takeoff (lb/kg)	12,566/5,700	18,390/8,342	20,065/9,100
Max external load (lb/kg)	5,600/2,540	6,800/3,084	6,800/3,084
Hardpoints	3	5	5
Power	Adour 151	Adour 861	Adour 871
Max (lb st/kN)	N/A	N/A	N/A
Mil (lb st/kN)	5,300/23.6	5,700/23.6	5,845/26.0
Fuel			
Internal (lb/kg)	2,849/1,293	2,927/1,330	2,927/1,330
External (lb/kg)	1,560/708	2,966/1,345	2,966/1,345
Fraction	0.27	0.26	0.24
Loadings			
Max thrust	N/A	N/A	N/A
Mil thrust	0.50 − 0.42	0.50 − 0.31	0.48 − 0.29
Wing clean to (lb/sq ft/kg/m²)	59/290	63/308	67/328
Wing max to (lb/sq ft/kg/m²)	70/341	102/499	111/544
Performance			
Vmax hi	M = 0.98	M = 0.98	M = 0.98
Vmax lo	M = 0.94	M = 0.94	M = 0.94
Ceiling (ft/m)	50,000/15,250	50,000/15,250	50,000/15,250
Initial climb (ft/min/m/sec)	6,000/30.5	9,300/47.0	12,000/61.0
Takeoff roll (ft/m)	2,000/610	2,000/610	2,000/610
Landing roll (ft/m)	2,000/610	1,900/580	1,900/580
First flight	21 Aug 1974	N/A	19 May 1986

in the Alpha Jet's favour, although it was also argued that two engines gave twice as much to go wrong.

As the Hawk matured, it demonstrated that its attrition rate was nothing like what had been projected, that its handling was superior and that its payload/range was far better. The final word can be left to the US Navy; when it evaluated contenders for its advanced trainer requirement it selected the Hawk, subject to its being made carrier-compatible by McDonnell Douglas, refusing to hold a competitive flyoff against the Alpha Jet on the grounds that it would be 'no contest'.

The use of armed trainers in the light attack and close support role is amost obligatory, and it would be a waste of a fast jet not to use it as such. The Hawk therefore underwent development resulting in the export Mk 50, which had improved avionics to the customer's requirements, the Adour Mk 851 engine with the same thrust but better acceleration, greater range, five hardpoints instead of the previous three, and maximum takeoff weight increased to 16,200lb (7,350kg). An optional braking parachute could also be fitted if requested.

The next stage was the Mk 60 series, which featured the more powerful Adour 861, an improved wing, air-to-air missile capability, and a maximum takeoff weight of 18,390lb (8,342kg); a braking parachute was standard on this series. Then came the Hawk 100 advanced ground attack aircraft, with an improved avionics fit, and an enhanced weapons management system. First flight of an aerodynamic prototype took place on 21 October 1987, and a steady flow of orders — primarily from current Hawk operators — are testimony to the type's potential.

A single-seat combat version of the Hawk, the Hawk 200, took to the air on 19 May 1986. A variety of avionics options are available, including an air-to-air radar or a chisel laser, nose, while two internal cannon with 150 rounds per gun free the centreline pylon for stores. On previous models it was usual to mount a gun pod in this position. Saudi Arabia is the lead customer for the type.

Depending on the exact avionics fit carried, the Hawk can operate with a wide variety of stores, including Sea Eagle. It has also proved itself to be no mean performer in the close combat air superiority areana.

Users

Abu Dhabi, Brunei, Dubai, Finland, Indonesia, Kenya, Kuwait, Oman, Saudi Arabia, South Korea, Switzerland, UK, USA, Zimbabwe

Below: The Hawk 200 is a single-seat light attack variant of the famous two-set trainer.

Fairchild A-10A Thunderbolt II

Type: Single-seat twin-engined close-air support fighter and "tankbuster".

The A-10A Thunderbolt II, more commonly known as the "Warthog", was originally conceived for the close air support mission, which involves the delivery of ordnance accurately in close proximity to friendly troops. Subsequently the requirement to kill tanks was introduced, the result being a big, slow flying gun which could double as a bomb truck.

Tactical Air Command (TAC) received the first of 721 A-10As in February 1976 and production continued until 1984. As well as TAC units based in the Continental USA, A-10As serve in Europe, South Korea and Alaska. In 1987, 26 OA-10A observation aircraft entered service with the 23rd Tactical Air Support Squadron (TASS). It is basically a standard A-10 but carries rockets to mark targets.

Drawing on experience from the Vietnam War, the A-10 was specifically designed for close air support (CAS)

Dimensions	A-10A Thunderbolt II
Length (ft/m)	53.33/16.26
Span (ft/m)	57.50/17.53
Height (ft/m)	14.67/4.47
Wing area (sq ft/m²)	506/47.02
Aspect ratio	6.53

Weights	
Empty (lb/kg)	21,519/9,760
Clean takeoff (lb/kg)	34,660/15,720
Max takeoff (lb/kg)	50,000/22,680
Max external load (lb/kg)	16,000/7,258
Hardpoints	11

Power	2 x TF34-GE-100 tf
Max (lb st/kN)	N/A
Mil (lb st/kN)	9,065/40.3

Fuel	
Internal (lb/kg)	10,650/4,830
External (lb/kg)	11,700/5,310
Fraction	0.31

Loadings	
Max thrust	N/A
Mil thrust	0.52 − 0.36
Wing clean to (lb/sq ft/kg/m²)	68/334
Wing max to (lb/sq ft/kg/m²)	99/482

Performance	
Vmax hi	M = 0.59
Vmax lo	M = 0.68
Ceiling (ft/m)	45,000/13,700
Initial climb (ft/min/m/sec)	6,000/30
Takeoff roll (ft/m)	4,000/1,220
Landing roll (ft/m)	2,000/610

First flight	May 1972 (prototype)

in a high threat environment, with a large warload, long loiter time and wide combat radius.

To allow the aircraft to take multiple hits from anti-aircraft fire and shoulder-launched surface-to-air missiles (SAMs), the cockpit was heavily armoured with titanium. Self-sealing fuel tanks are standard, the hydraulic system has a manual back up and the engines are outside the fuselage body. This positioning allows for one powerplant to be lost to a heat-seeking SAM and the aircraft to keep flying.

Iron, cluster and laser-guided bombs can be carried, but the A-10's main guided weapon is Maverick, which employs electro-optical guidance and gives some stand-off capability; the latest version of Maverick, with IR guidance, entered service in 1986. The A-10's main weapon, however, is its gigantic 30mm GAU-8/A Avenger seven-barrelled cannon, around which the aircraft was designed. This gun system has an ammunition capacity of 1,174 rounds, and two rates of fire are available: 2,100 or 4,200 rounds per minute. The muzzle velocity of 3,500ft/sec (1,067m/sec) is very high, and aids accuracy.

Its CAS mission meant that the A-10A had to be able to operate from unprepared forward operating locations.

Below: An A-10A turns tightly just above the treetops.

During its service with the USAF, the A-10A has never been truly popular with the "top brass", who preferred faster, sleeker and more expensive aircraft. By 1990 the USAF had even proposed scrapping the A-10 in favour of the A-16 ground attack version of the Fighting Falcon.

The success of the A-10A during Operations *Desert Storm* and *Provide Comfort*, however, firmly quashed these moves and the ugly "Warthog" is now firmly back in favour in the Pentagon.

First to arrive in Saudi Arabia, during August 1991, were the A-10As of the 345th Tactical Fighter Wing's (TFW) 353rd and 355th Tactical Fighter Squadrons (TFS). Soon afterwards, the 75th and 76th TFS' of the 23rd TFW joined them at King Fahd Airport, near Damman. The Desert Warthog's were known as the *Fahd Squad*. In November 1990, US President George Bush ordered the American forces in the Middle East to be doubled and more A-10As were soon on their way to King Fahd. The 511th TFS from the 10th TFW and the 706th TFW from the Air Force Reserve flew their A-10As out to join the *Fahd Squad* in November. 12 OA-10As from the 23rd TASS arrived in December to bring the total number of A-10As in the Middle East to 144.

In the first hours of *Desert Storm*, A-10As were in action agaisnt Iraqi early warning radars. Attention then started to be switched further behind the Iraqi frontline, with armour, artillery, SAMs, supply dumps and other battlefield air interdiction targets being hit with 30mm cannon fire, 500lb (227kg) and 2,000lb (908kg) bombs, cluster bombs and Maverick missiles.

Eventually the A-10As were attacking the Iraqi Republican Guard around the clock, often with the help of air-refuelling to boost their loiter time. Infra-red and television-guided versions of the Maverick missile were

Below: The A-10A was designed from the outset to be able to operate from short airstrips, thus permitting this rugged performer to be forward based closer to the enemy front line. This ability was used to good effect during the Gulf War.

fired to great effect and accounted for the majority of the 1,000 A-10A tank "kills" during the war. Some 2,000 other military vehicles and 1,200 artillery pieces fell victim to the Warthogs by the end of the conflict.

Warthogs took heavy punishment during their missions over Kuwait and southern Iraq. More than 70 came back to base with battle damage, including massive holes in wings. The majority were soon repaired and back in action. The Warthog was the plane the Iraqi soldiers feared the most because its long endurance and heavy armour meant it was able to loiter over the battlefield looking for targets, while fast jets usually would make one pass and then speed back to base. Its long endurance was also put to the test in the hunt for Scud missiles in western Iraq, where they flew long patrols to stop the missiles being moved along roads by daylight.

After the war the Warthogs of the 81st TFW were used to help the Kurdish relief effort, acting as scouts for C-130 transports carrying relief supplies. The Warthogs flew ahead of the C-130s to find groups of refugees and then guided the Hercules into their drop zones. Later the Warthogs flew combat air patrols over the Kurdish "safe haven" to protect the relief effort from Iraqi interference.

With the A-10A now back in favour with the USAF, major improvements have been made to the aircraft's capabilities. About 90 have been given radar altimeters, ground proximity warning systems, more accurate bomb sights, modified flight controls and air-to-air aiming for the 30mm cannon, under the Low Altitude Safety and Targeting Enhancement (LASTE) programme. Other improvements under consideration include fitting FLIR and a GPS terminal.

User
USA

Below: Though it is ungainly in appearance (for which it has earned the nickname of "Warthog"), the A-10A can turn on a sixpence — vital if it is to evade anti-aircraft fire when making an attack at below treetop level.

General Dynamics F-16 Fighting Falcon

Type: Single-seat single-engined fighter, developed initially for the air superiority role but since adopted as a swing fighter able to switch from air combat to attack as needed. Variants include fully combat-capable two-seaters with slightly less fuel.

When the F-16 Fighting Falcon is mentioned, the usual reaction is to think of it as a fighter with unparalleled capability in close combat. It originated with the Lightweight Fighter (LWF) proposal in the early 1970s, won a much publicised flyoff against the Northrop YF-17, and was adopted as an air combat fighter by the USAF and subsequently by many other nations. It has received wide publicity in its designated role, with particular attention being paid to its ability to sustain a 9g turn, although that is possible in only a small section of the flight envelope.

Its attack capability has received less attention; attacking surface

Dimensions	F-16A	F-16C	F-16C MSIP
Length (ft/m)	49.25/15.01	49.25/15.01	49.25/15.01
Span (ft/m)	31.00/9.45	31.00/9.45	31.00/9.45
Height (ft/m)	16.58/5.05	16.58/5.05	16.58/5.05
Wing area (sq ft/m²)	300/27.88	300/27.88	300/27.88
Aspect ratio	3.20	3.20	3.20
Weights			
Empty (lb/kg)	16,234/7,364	17,960/8,150	17,960/8,150
Clean takeoff (lb/kg)	23,810/10,800	26,536/12,040	26,536/12,040
Max takeoff (lb/kg)	35,400/16,057	37,500/17,010	37,500/17,010
Max external load (lb/kg)	15,200/6,895	15,200/6,895	15,200/6,895
Hardpoints	7	7	7
Power	F100-PW-100 tf	F100-PW-100 tf	F100-GE-400 or F100-220
Max (lb st/kN)	23,904/106.3	23,904/106.3	28,000/124.5
Mil (lb st/kN)	14,780/65.7	14,780/65.7	17,000/75.6
Fuel			
Internal (lb/kg)	6,972/3,162	6,972/3,162	6,972/3,162
External (lb/kg)	6,760/3,066	6,760/3,066	6,760/3,066
Fraction	0.29	0.26	0.26
Loadings			
Max thrust	1.00−0.68	0.90−0.64	1.06−0.75
Mil thrust	0.62−0.42	0.57−0.39	0.64−0.45
Wing clean to (lb/sq ft/kg/m²)	79/387	88/432	88/432
Wing max to (lb/sq ft/kg/m²)	118/576	125/610	125/610
Performance			
Vmax hi	M = 2.0	M = 2.0	M = 2.0
Vmax lo	M = 1.2	M = 1.2	M = 1.2
Ceiling (ft/m)	50,000/15,250	50,000/15,250	50,000/15,250
Initial climb (ft/min/m/sec)	50,000/254	50,000/254	50,000/254
Takeoff roll (ft/m)	1,750/533	1,750/533	1,750/533
Landing roll (ft/m)	2,650/808	2,650/808	2,650/808
First flight	20 Jan 1974	19 June 1984	N/A

targets does not carry the glamour of air combat, but in fact this role is of hardly less significance to F-16 operators than air superiority. Designed originally as an austere close combat fighter, to add numerical strength to the USAF's relatively small numbers of F-15s, the Fighting Falcon was given considerable ground attack capability at an early development stage. This facility earned it the name of the swing fighter: air superiority was to be gained by a combination of F-15s and F-16s, whereupon the F-16 could be switched to ground targets. That is an oversimplification: air superiority can be considerably assisted by attacks on enemy airfields and other air assets on the ground,

and the exact point at which the F-16 ceases to operate as an air combat fighter and reverts to the attack role is a matter for the commander of operations on the spot.

The F-16 is a small fighter, and for air combat carries an internal 20mm M61 Vulcan cannon with 500 rounds and two Sidewinders mounted on wingtip rails. This basic weapons fit is retained for the air-to-ground mission to give some defensive capability on the outward leg, and turn it into what amounts to a sweeping fighter on the return trip, needing little or no fighter escort.

Below: Four "slicks" fall away from an F-16A Fighting Falcon.

Right: A quartet of US Air Force F-16C Fighting Falcons give an indication of their dual-role air superiority/ground attack capabilities, courtesy of wingtip-mounted AIM-9 Sidewinder air-to-air missiles and underwing-mounted cluster bomb units.

Some idea of the importance of the attack mission can be gained from the rather basic APG-66 radar fitted to the F-16A and B, which had no fewer than seven air-to-ground modes. These included real-beam ground mapping, expanded real-beam ground mapping, Doppler beam sharpening, air-to-ground ranging and surface search and freeze, the last of which enables the picture on the plan position indicator in the cockpit to remain the same as on the last sweep, showing the aircraft's progress across the screen and allowing the radar to be put on standby until next needed.

The high thrust to weight ratio and moderate wing loading in clean condition allowed an external payload to be carried that was nearly equivalent to the empty weight of the aircraft, while the use of relaxed static stability coupled with fly-by-wire reduced handling problems at high all-up weights and ensured that the pilot could not overstress the aircraft in heavy manoeuvring. Naturally the 9g sustained turn was impossible with the pylons laden, being reduced to a limit of 5.5g instantaneous, which is still better than most loaded attack aircraft can manage. The two-seat F-16B has comparable performance to the A-model except in radius of action, the space for the second crew position being achieved at a cost of some 1,187lb (538kg) of fuel.

Inevitably, the F-16 was upgraded, the next variants to appear being the F-16C and D, with the much more capable APG-68 radar and upgraded avionics, which increased the empty weight. A three-phase Multi-Stage Improvement Programme (MSIP) is currently adding an even better avionics fit and more powerful engines, either Pratt & Whitney's F100-220 or General Electric's F110-400, which will restore the F-16C's reduced thrust loadings to better than those of the original F-16A.

Figting Falcons have seen extensive action in USAF, Israeli and Pakistani service. Eight F-16s led the Israeli bombing raid on the Iraqi Osirak nuclear reactor in June 1981. A year later Israeli Fighting Falcons were heavily engaged in the air battles with the Syrian Air Force over Lebanon. During these battles the F-16 demonstrated both its superb bombing accuracy and deadly dogfighting capability. Israeli F-16s have been extensively modified to carry electronic warfare equipment to counter surface-to-air missile radars.

During the mid-1980s Pakistani Air Force F-16A/Bs fought many air battles with Soviet and Afghan aircraft along Pakistan's northern border, claiming several MiGs in the process.

The Gulf War saw the biggest combat test of the Fighting Falcon, when the USAF deployed 249 F-16s to the Middle East. The USAF's 50th, 52nd, 347th, 363rd, 388th and 401st Tactical Fighter Wings (TFW) took F-16C/Ds to bases in Saudi Arabia, Turkey and the Gulf States. Further F-16/Bs of the New York and South Carolina Air National Guard, were deployed to Al Kharj in Saudi Arabia.

USAF F-16s were used primarily for bombing missions against targets deep in Iraq and in the Kuwaiti theatre of operations, flying some 13,500 combat sorties — the highest for any type of aircraft during Operation *Desert Storm*. A wide range of targets were attacked, including airfields,

chemical and nuclear plants, supply convoys, Scud missile sites and Iraqi Army units. Most F-16 units demonstrated the inherent flexibility of the aircraft by taking on all the different missions required.

Some squadrons, however, specialised to a certain degree, with the 23rd Tactical Fighter Squadron (TFS), of the 52nd TFW, concentrating on supporting the Wing's own F-4G Wild Weasels in their campaign against Iraqi air defences. The two Air National Guard Squadrons took on a disproportionate amount of the battlefield preparation work, attacking frontline Iraqi positions and the Repubican Guard. Night attack missions fell to the 388th TFW which had the only F-16 LANTIRN navigation pods available in the Middle East. F-16s from the unit also flew as Fast-Forward Air Controllers , or "Killer Scouts", patrolling over the Kuwaiti battlefield, looking for targets and then guiding other aircraft to attack them.

The USAF had taken delivery of 1,583 F-16s by 1990 and had a further 1,000 aircraft on order. Some 1,300 have been ordered or delivered to foreign buyers. During its production, on-going improvements have been made to each block of aircraft, with the current F-16C/D Block 50 aircraft featuring higher thrust engines, improved avionics and armament provision. Later upgrades are also to include provision for the new "smart" HARM anti-radar missile. A number of projects are underway to develop the next multi-role fighter to enter service early in the 21st Century. Ideas include the Falcon 21 and Agile Falcon, which feature vastly improved avionics and new wing shapes.

Users

Bahrain, Belgium, Denmark, Egypt, Greece, Indonesia, Israel, Netherlands, Norway, Pakistan, Singapore, South Korea, Thailand, Turkey, USA, Venezuela.

Below: Operational roles for the F-16 include that of maritime strike. This Norwegian F-16A carries a pair of Penguin Mk 3 anti-shipping missiles.

General Dynamics F-111

Type: Two-seat twin-engined all-weather long-range interdiction and strike bomber. Other variants are the EF-111A electronic warfare aircraft (F-111A rebuilt by Grumman) and the RF-111C operated by the Royal Australian Air Force.

The F-111 started life in the early 1960s as a multi-role aircraft for both the USAF and US Navy. Costs and technical limitations put paid to the "Aardvark" — as the F-111 was nicknamed — entering US Navy service. Plans for the UK to buy it for the Royal Air Force were also scrapped because of cost. Only the USAF and the Royal Australian Air Force eventually bought the F-111.

It was the first variable-geometry aircraft to enter frontline service with any air force. More significant, from an operational point of view, was the F-111's pioneering of low-level deep penetration tactics using terrain-following radar during the Vietnam War. More recently, the success of the F-111F's Pave Tack laser designation system during the Gulf War was a major factor in the aerial victory.

Dimensions	F-111AE	F-111F	FB-111A
Length (ft/m)	75.54/23.02	75.54/23.02	75.58/23.04
Span (ft/m)	63.00/19.20 max	63.00/19.20 max	70.00/21.33 max
Height (ft/m)	17.04/5.19	17.04/5.19	17.04/5.19
Wing area (sq ft/m²)	525/48.79 max	525/48.79 max	550/51.11 max
Aspect ratio	7.56 − 1.95	7.56 − 1.95	8.91 − 2.10
Weights			
Empty (lb/kg)	46,172/20,940	47,481/21,540	47,980/21,760
Clean takeoff (lb/kg)	79,366/36,000	80,640/36,580	84,957/38,535
Max takeoff (lb/kg)	91,300/41,400	100,000/45,360	119,243/54,090
Max external load (lb/kg)	19,800/8,980	19,800/8,980	19,800/8,980
Hardpoints	4	4	4
Power	2 x TF30-3 tf	2 x TF30-100 tf	2 x TF30-7 tf
Max (lb st/kN)	18,500/82.2	25,100/111.5	20,350/90.4
Mil (lb st/kN)	12,500/55.6	14,500/64.4	12,500/55.6
Fuel			
Internal (lb/kg)	32,715/14,840	32,660/14,815	36,477/16,545
External (lb/kg)	15,613/7,080	15,613/7,080	23,418/10,620
Fraction	0.41	0.41	0.43
Loadings			
Max thrust	0.47 − 0.41	0.62 − 0.50	0.48 − 0.34
Mil thrust	0.31 − 0.27	0.36 − 0.29	0.29 − 0.21
Wing clean to (lb/sq ft/kg/m²)	151/738	154/750	154/750
Wing max to (lb/sq ft/kg/m²)	174/849	190/930	217/1,058
Performance			
Vmax hi	M = 2.2	M = 2.5	M = 2.1
Vmax lo	M = 1.2	M = 1.2	M = 1.2
Ceiling (ft/m)	51,000/15,550	60,000/18,275	51,000/15,550
Initial climb (ft/min/m/sec)	N/A	N/A	N/A
Takeoff roll (ft/m)	N/A	N/A	N/A
Landing roll (ft/m)	N/A	N/A	N/A
First flight	Dec 1964/ Aug 1969	Aug 1971	30 July 1967

The first versions of the F-111 entered service with the USAF from 1968 and were soon committed to action in Vietnam. Heavy combat losses resulted in the early F-111As being withdrawn from South-East Asia after only a few months. They were recommitted in 1972 and proved more successful during the "Linebreaker II" air offensive. The F-111As continued to serve with the 366th Tactical Fighter Wing (TFW) at Mountain Home Air Force base, Idaho, until 1991, when they were retired.

The improved F-111E model served in the Continental USA before deploying to RAF Upper Heyford in the UK with the 20th TFW. One of its squadrons, the 79th Tactical Fighter Squadron (TFS), saw service during the Gulf War, flying from Turkey.

Strategic Air Command received some 75 FB-111A which were optimised for the delivery of nuclear weapons. They were retired by 1991, except for 18 which are being converted to F-111G standard for use by Tactical Air Command.

The most successful version is the F-111F which is fitted with the Pave Tack laser designating pod in the fuselage bomb bay. F-111Fs from the 48th TFW based at RAF Lakenheath in the UK gave the Pave Tack system its combat debut in 1986, when they bombed the Libyan capital of Tripoli. Some 66 aircraft deployed from the UK to Saudi Arabia in late 1990. During Operation *Desert Storm* the 48th TFW dropped 7.3 million pounds (3.17 million kg) of precision-guided munitions, including GBU-15 2,000lb (908kg) electro-optical guided bombs and the newly developed GBU-28 deep penetration bomb. Under USAF re-organisation plans, the 48th TFW is to lose its F-111Fs from 1992 and the 27th TFW at Cannon Air Force Base, New Mexico, is to become the sole operator of the type.

The final version developed is the EF-111A Raven electronic warfare aircraft. EF-111As from RAF Upper Heyford and Mountain Home Air Force Base, Idaho, served during Operation *Desert Storm*, specialising in jamming Iraqi early warning radars.

Users
Australia, USA

Below: A dozen Mk 82 500lb (227kg) practice bombs fall away from an F-111D's racks.

Above: An F-111A of the 366th TFW, seen over the Nellis AFB ranges with a full load of 24 Mk 82 500lb (227kg) "slicks" carried on "six-pack" racks.

Below: Tripoli, April 14 1986: Ilyushin Il-76 transports as seen by Pave Tack on an F-111F three seconds (upper) and one second (lower) from impact.

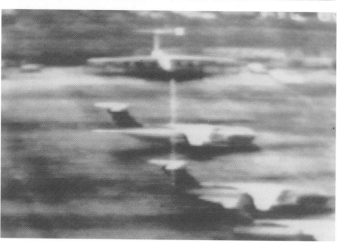

Below: An Il-76 caught in the crosshairs just one second (upper) from impact. Then the Pave Tack head turns (lower) to show nine bombs on descent.

Above: An F-111F with a Pave Tack targeting pod mounted on the centreline and a quartet of Paveway laser-guided bombs on the underwing stations.

Grumman A-6 Intruder

Type: Two-seat all-weather carrier-based attack bomber. Variants are the KA-6 tanker and the EA-6 Prowler four-seat electronic warfare aircraft.

In photographs the Grumman A-6 Intruder has a curiously innocuous look. Its portly but gracefully curving fuselage, the high aspect ratio, almost unswept wing, and the 'Mickey Mouse' divided windshield, combine to give it the appearance of a warplane designed under the auspices of the Disney Studios. But photographs can be deceptive; in real life the Intruder is impressively large

for a carrier-based aircraft and gives an abiding impression of solidity, an impression that is confirmed by its record to date.

The origins of the Intruder lie in a late 1950s US Marine Corps requirement for an aircraft that could hit targets of opportunity at night or in marginal weather conditions. The requirement, born of experience in Korea, was intended to produce an aircraft able to locate reinforcements being brought up under conditions that precluded orthodox air attack and accurately place ordnance on them, capable of adverse-weather close support and carrier-compat-

Dimensions	A-6E Intruder
Length (ft/m)	54.75 / 16.69
Span (ft/m)	53.00 / 16.15
Height (ft/m)	16.16 / 4.93
Wing area (sq ft/m²)	529 / 49.15
Aspect ratio	5.31

Weights	
Empty (lb/kg)	26,600 / 12,090
Clean takeoff (lb/kg)	43,000 / 19,500
Max takeoff (lb/kg)	58,600 / 26,580
Max external load (lb/kg)	18,000 / 8,165
Hardpoints	6

Power	
	2 x J52-8B tj
Max (lb st/kN)	N/A
Mil (lb st/kN)	9,300 / 41.4

Fuel	
Internal (lb/kg)	15,939 / 7,230
External (lb/kg)	10,050 / 4,558
Fraction	0.37

Loadings	
Max thrust	0.43 — 0.32
Mil thrust	N/A
Wing clean to (lb/sq ft/kg/m²)	81 / 397
Wing max to (lb/sq ft/kg/m²)	111 / 541

Performance	
Vmax hi	M = 0.94
Vmax lo	M = 0.85
Ceiling (ft/m)	42,400 / 12,900
Initial climb (ft/min/m/sec)	8,600 / 44
Takeoff roll (ft/m)	4,560 / 1,390
Landing roll (ft/m)	2,540 / 774

First flight	1970

ible. Long range and/or extended loiter time were necessary, dictating the high fuel fraction, though at that time such things as fuel fractions had not been thought of.

The mainly low-level attack profile called for was at odds with the low-speed needs of carrier operations; the latter took priority and Grumman settled for a large-span, high-aspect-ratio wing with a high lift coefficient and flaps to almost the entire leading and trailing edges; lateral control was by spoilers. Most unusually, the air brakes are situated on the wingtips and are of a split type, the upper and lower surfaces of the trailing edge opening up and down respectively. Typical approach speed is 120kt (222km/h) and stall speed at normal landing weight is just under 100kt (185km/h).

The Intruder has been built in several different variants. The original A-6A, equipped with digital integrated attack navigation equipment (DIANE), saw extensive service in Vietnam, flying approximately 35,000 combat missions with both Navy and Marine Corps, the Navy aircraft being carrier-based while the Marine Corps aircraft were based on land at Da Nang and Chu Lai. DIANE was both expensive and unreliable, two factors which contributed to a lack of enough Intruders to perform

Below: Five weapons attachment points allow the A-6E to lift up to 18,000lb (8,165kg) of ordnance.

all the tasks called for. The expense had resulted in a low acquisition rate, and Intruder squadrons represented only one in five of the fixed-wing squadrons making up the complement of a carrier, while squadron establishment was at first fixed at only nine aircraft (later increased to a dozen).

The unreliability of DIANE was caused by the primitive level of technology, and at one point aircraft serviceability was down to a mere 35 per cent. On the other hand, when it worked it worked very well. The USMC squadrons had an advantage in that they could equip forward air controllers with radar beacons, which gave a precise point on the ground from which the Intruders could offset their attacks. Navy Intruders were used from 1965 until the end of the war in 1973, often on deep penetration strikes and frequently in the monsoon season, when no other type could operate. A total of 65 Intruders were lost to enemy action over Vietnam, 47 of them Navy aircraft, but only two were lost to MiGs, both in 1967.

The need to counter the Vietnamese SAM systems gave rise to a defence suppression variant, the A-6B, 19 of which were converted from A-6As to carry the AGM-78 Standard anti-radiation missile. Night attacks against small moving targets such as trucks called for improved detection capability, and a dozen A-6As were fitted with FLIR and LLTV equipment in small turrets under a programme called TRIM (Trails,

Above: In service with both the US Navy and Marine Corps for nearly three decades, the A-6 Intruder has proved to be a faithful "bomb truck".

Roads, Interdiction, Multisensor), being redesignated A-6C, and a specialised tanker variant, the KA-6D, was also developed.

In the meantime an electronic warfare aircraft developed from the Intruder, the EA-6A, was an interim design introduced to service in 1967, and only 19 were produced before it was replaced by the greatly modified and far more capable EA-6B Prowler, which had two extra seats to accommodate Electronic Warfare Officers and was packed with electronic detection and jamming gear.

The current variant of the Intruder is the A-6E. The first deliveries began in 1971, and the changes were mainly to the avionics with the dual goal of improving both capability and serviceability. The two radars of the A-6A were replaced by a single Norden APQ-148 multi-mode radar, with track-while-scan, terrain avoidance and ground mapping modes, while solid-state electronics were introduced, including a new computer and a new nav/attack system. The overall effect was dramatic: system serviceability increased to an average of 85 per cent, navigational accuracy was increased by one third, and bombing Circular Error Probability (CEP) was nearly halved in the radar aiming mode and more than halved in the visual mode. In addition to the new production A-6Es a total of 240 A-6As were converted to the new operational standard.

In 1976 Target Recognition Attack Multisensor (TRAM) was introduced. The TRAM system contained an imaging infra-red (IIR) sensor, a laser ranger/designator and a laser spot tracker housed in a small turret beneath the radome. The IIR sensor gives a television-quality picture of the target which is displayed on a screen mounted directly above the radar display; capable of considerable magnification, it is an invaluable aid to target recognition and identification when operating at night.

The A-6E has been the workhorse of US carrier airpower throughout the 1980s. Its combat debut was not very auspicious, when one was lost to Syrian air defences during a daytime raid over the Lebanon in 1983. Intruders and Prowlers from the USS' *Coral Sea* and *America* were more successul three years later when they spearheaded the air assault on Libya.

Operation *Desert Storm* saw around 150 US Navy and US Marine Corps A-6Es, EA-6Bs and KA-6Ds playing a key role in all aspects of the Coalition air offensive against Iraq. HARM-armed Prowlers and Intruders were involved in the decisive attack on Baghdad's air defences in the opening hours of the war. In subsequent attacks the Prowler/HARM combination was used to great effect by both the US Navy and USMC to protect Coalition strike packages.

Using TRAM, US Navy A-6Es were able to deliver laser-guided bombs on to strategic Iraqi targets with pin-point accuracy. During the latter stages of the war they progressed to using their laser-guided bombing capability to destroy Iraqi tanks and artillery positions in Kuwait. Intruders from the USS' *Ranger, Midway, America* and *Theodore Roosevelt* were very active against Iraqi naval forces in the northern Arabian Gulf. To boost the number of strike aircraft available to attack Iraq, the US Navy re-shuffled their Intruder force to deploy 24 A-6E/KA-6Ds (almost double the usual complement) on three of its carriers — the USS' *Ranger, Midway* and *Theodore Roosevelt*.

USMC Intruders, flown by VMA (AW)-224 and -533 and operating from Bahrain, were heavily involved in the 3rd Marine Air Wing's interdiction and close air support campaign against the Iraqi Army. EA-6Bs of VMAQ-2 were airborne around the clock to support USMC strike aircraft attacking Iraqi targets in Kuwait.

With the cancellation in 1991 of the A-12 Stealth Attack Aircraft, the US Navy's plans to replace the A-6E were thrown into considerable disarray. The US Navy now plans to replace its A-6Es with the new AX, but it will not enter service until the next century so it is proposed to re-wing many Intruders to extend their service life.

User
USA

Below: A variety of air-to-surface missiles can also be carried by the Intruder, as exemplified by the AGM-136A Tacit Rainbow anti-radar missile aboard this A-6E.

Lockheed F-117A Stealth Fighter

Type: Single-seat precision night-strike aircraft. No other variants have been acknowledged, but rumours persist that a specialist reconnaissance version is in service.

The Lockheed F-117A Stealth Fighter is the world's first operational combat aircraft designed to exploit "low observable" or so-called "stealth" technology. Its distinctive angular shape is now legendary thanks to the black jet's exploits over Baghdad in the opening hours of the Gulf War.

Development of the F-117A dates back to the mid-1970s when a number of US aerospace companies were experimenting with various technologies designed to defeat Soviet radar and surface-to-air missile defences. In 1978, Lockheed's Advanced Development Projects facility at Burbank, California, nicknamed the "Skunk Works", was awarded a Pentagon contract to turn an advanced demonstrator, codenamed *HAVE BLUE*, into an operational precision strike aircraft. Using the expertise developed on the U-2 and SR-71 projects, Lockheed's team were able to get the first F-117A airborne in only 31 months.

Tactical Air Command received the first of its F-117As in 1982 and its first combat unit, the 4450th Tactical Group, achieved initial operational capability in October 1983 at Tonopah Test Range in Nevada.

The F-117A employs a variety of technologies to mask it from detection by enemy radar. Firstly, it is coated in radar-absorbent material (RAM) which is intended to "soak up" radar energy. Secondly, the angular shape of the aircraft plays havoc with the reflection of radar energy by using a technique known as "faceting". Thirdly, a special "platypus" exhaust system cuts down on the amount of heat energy given off by the aircraft's turbofan engines. The internal design of the F-117A is just as important to the aircraft's stealth capabilities as its external characteristics. This is one area that remains highly classified and expert speculation suggests that RAM

Dimensions	Lockheed F-117A
Length (ft/m)	65.95/20.1
Span (ft/m)	43.3/13.2
Height (ft/m)	12.45/3.78
Wing area (ft²/m²)	c.1,140/105.9

Weights	
Empty (lb/kg)	29,500/13,380
Loaded (lb/kg)	c.48,000/21,800
Max (lb/kg)	52,750/23,926
Max internal load (lb/kg)	5,000/2,267
Hardpoints	all stores internal

Power	2 x GE F-404 F1D2 tf
Max (lb st/kN)	c.12,000/5,440

Fuel	
Internal (lb/kg)	c.17,000/7,711
Fraction	c.0.35

Performance	"High subsonic"

First flight	18 June 1981

is used throughout the F-117's internal compartments, with its engines receiving particular attention to cut down their radar reflections.

Although generally referred to as the Stealth Fighter, the F-117A has no air-to-air capability or self-defence systems, such as jammers, chaff or flare dispensers. It relies on its stealth technology and the cover of darkness to avoid enemy fighters and air defences. The F-117A's armament is optimised for precision night attack, with forward- and downard-looking infra-red sensors used to direct precision-guided munitions onto their targets. Primary weapons are the Paveway series GBU-10 and GBU-27 laser-guided bombs. An inertial navigation system enables the F-117A to find targets deep in enemy territory while flying at night.

During the early years of its existence, the F-117A was classified as a "black" programme. Development work, production, deployment and operational details were all highly secret. The aircraft were only allowed to fly at night and when two crashed, extraordinary measures were taken to prevent unauthorised access to the crash sites.

In 1988 the USAF declassified the F-117A to some extent and examples were shown off to a curious press and public. It is believed that the strain of night flying on the trainee pilots was behind the public unveiling: from now on new pilots could learn to fly the aircraft in the relative safety of daylight. The following year the 4450th Tactical Group was redesignated the 37th Tactical Fighter Wing (TFW). Three squadrons form the Wing: the 415th Tactical Fighter Squadron ("The Nightstalkers"); the 416th TFS ("The Ghostriders"); and the 417th Tactical Fighter Training Squadron ("The Bandits"). The latter squadron is responsible for training new F-117A pilots. US Budget cuts in 1990 have led the USAF to propose that the Wing and its 59 Stealth Fighters move to Holloman Air Force base in New Mexico from 1992.

Reports suggest that the US Joint Chiefs-of-Staff considered using the F-117A in 1983 to strike targets in Lebanon and three years later to assist in the US revenge strike on Libya, but concern for secrecy prevented the Stealth Fighter being launched into action. However, six F-117As were sent

Below: Quite unlike any other fighter, past or present, the Lockheed F-117A manages to look sleek despite a mass of sharp angles. Note the total absence of external pylons.

Above: The full mission capabilities of the F-117A have yet to be revealed, but its performance over downtown Baghdad with laser-guided "smart" bombs left no-one in any doubt as to its effectiveness in the air-to-ground role.

into action on 19 December 1989 in support of the US invasion of Panama. Laser-guided bombs were dropped into a field next to a Panamanian Army barracks at Rio Hato. Controversy still surround the attack, with the USAF claiming the F-117As were only trying to scare the Panamanians into surrender, while less charitable observers questioned the bombing accuracy of the Stealth Fighter.

A few months later the F-117A was put under a rather more intensive spotlight, when the 37th TFW deployed to Saudi Arabia as part of Operation *Desert Shield*. First to move was the 415th TFS, which deployed 18 F-117As to Khamis Mushait in southwest Saudi Arabia on 19 August 1990, with the aid of air-to-air refuelling. In December, the 416th TFS folowed its sister squadron to Khamis Mushait, or "Tonopah East" as the base was dubbed by F-117A pilots. The 417th TFTS sent a further six F-117As out to Saudi Arabia in January 1991, just after the start of Operation *Desert Storm*.

F-117As spearheaded the USAF air offensive against Iraq, hitting key targets in Baghdad in the first minutes of the war before the enemy's air defences had been suppressed. Other F-117As took out vital air defence sites on the border with Saudi Arabia to allow conventional aircraft to strike into Iraq. Throughout the war the F-117As struck at numerous targets in Iraq without being detected or fired at by the enemy air defences. Targets attacked included key communications centres; research, development, production and storage facilities for nuclear and chemical weapons; numerous hardened aircraft shelters; bridges, railroad choke points, major highways and Iraqi defence systems in Kuwait. More controversial was an attack on 13 February against a hardened bunker in Baghdad that contained hundreds of civilians. Coalition military spokesmen at the time claimed the F-117A's target was a command and control facility, but other officers later admitted that their intelligence might have been faulty.

The F-117A was the workhorse of the Coalition's strategic air campaign, the 42 aircraft in-theatre flying more than 1,200 combat sorties, over 6,900 combat hours and delivering more

Above: For what is quite a large aircraft, a pair of LGBs can best be described as a modest weapons load.

Right: A closer inspection of the F-117A emphasises the sharp angles adopted throughout to enhance radar reflection.

than 2,000 tons of ordnance with pinpoint accuracy.

USAF chiefs have dubbed the F-117A the "stellar performer" of the war, pointing to the fact that the Stealth Fighters represented only 2.5 per cent of the USAF aircraft in-theatre but were responsible for 40 per cent of the targets destroyed.

In late 1991, Lockheed proposed to extend the life of the F-117A by upgrading the existing aircraft to F-117A + standard by replacing their GE F404s with the GE F412 engines developed for the now-defunct US Navy A-12 Stealth Attack Aircraft. Other modifictions include improved stealth capabilities, new all-weather sensors, low probability of intercept communications systems, integrated global positioning navigation receivers and increasing the mission radius from 570nm (1,056km) to 730nm (1,353km). Lockheed is also working on an F-117B which includes provision for extra fuel to extend the aircraft's range and doubles its payload. However, no funding has been approved for either project to date.

User
USA

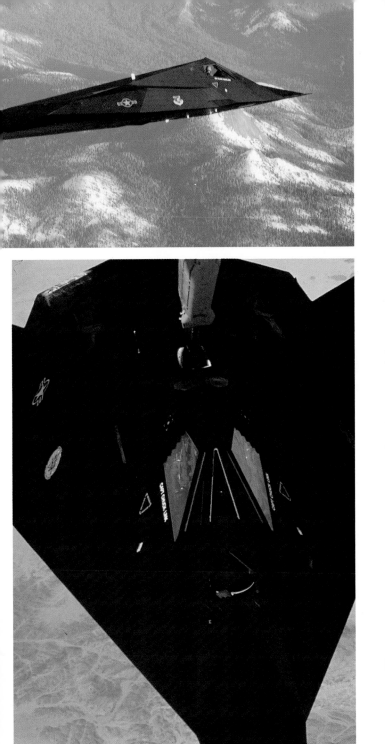

McDonnell Douglas F-4 Phantom II

Type: Two-seat twin-engined multi-role fighter employed primarily in the attack role but still used by some countries as an interceptor/air superiority fighter; reconnaissance versions have been developed and the USAF has a Wild Weasel defence suppression variant.

The veteran F-4 Phantom II first entered frontline service in the early 1960s and looks set to soldier on until the end of the decade and possibly into the next century. Its power and rugged construction have made it one of the 20th Century's most successful combat aircraft, with more than 5,000 rolling off McDonnell Douglas's St Louis production line. American Phantoms saw combat in Vietnam and the Gulf, while Israeli Air Force F-4s have seen extensive action since 1969. Iran has also used F-4s in combat.

Over the past decade the US military has steadily been replacing the F-4, but it is proving to be a hard act to follow. F-16s and F-15Es have taken its place in USAF strike

Dimensions	F-4E	F-4F	F-4G
Length (ft/m)	63.00/19.20	63.00/19.20	63.00/19.20
Span (ft/m)	38.33/11.68	38.33/11.68	38.33/11.68
Height (ft/m)	16.25/4.95	16.25/4.95	16.25/4.95
Wing area (sq ft/m²)	530/49.25	530/49.25	530/49.25
Aspect ratio	2.77	2.77	2.77
Weights			
Empty (lb/kg)	29,535/13,400	28,400/12,880	31,000/14,060
Clean takeoff (lb/kg)	43,150/19,570	41,400/18,780	44,600/20,230
Max takeoff (lb/kg)	61,795/28,030	60,630/27,500	61,795/28,030
Max external load (lb/kg)	18,645/8,460	19,230/8,720	17,200/7,800
Hardpoints	9	7	9
Power			
Max (lb st/kN)	2 x J79-17 tj	2 x J79-17 tj	2xJ79-17 tj
Mil (lb st/kN)	17,900/79.5	17,900/79.5	17,900/79.5
	11,870/52.8	11,870/52.8	11,870/52.8
Fuel			
Internal (lb/kg)	13,020/5,900	12,400/5,625	13,020/5,625
External (lb/kg)	8,710/3,950	8,710/3,950	8,710/3,950
Fraction	0.30	0.30	0.30
Loadings			
Max thrust	0.83 – 0.58	0.86 – 0.59	0.80 – 0.58
Mil thrust	0.55 – 0.38	0.57 – 0.39	0.53 – 0.38
Wing clean to (lb/sq ft/kg/m²)	81/398	78/381	84/411
Wing max to (lb/sq ft/kg/m²)	117/569	114/559	117/569
Performance			
Vmax hi	M = 2 +	M = 2 +	M = 2 +
Vmax lo	M = 1.19	M = 1.19	M = 1.19
Ceiling (ft/m)	55,000/16,750	55,000/16,750	55,000/16,750
Initial climb (ft/min/m/sec)	28,000/142	28,000/142	28,000/142
Takeoff roll (ft/m)	3,300/1,000	3,300/1,000	3,300/1,000
Landing roll (ft/m)	3,100/950	3,100/950	3,100/950
First flight	Aug 1965	May 1973	Dec 1975

squadrons, but a satisfactory replacement has yet to be found for the USAF's reconnaissance RF-4Cs and F-4G Wild Weasel defence suppression aircraft. The US Navy has fully replaced the F-4 in the fleet defence role with the F-14 Tomcat. US Marine Corps (USMC) fighter/strike squadrons have traded their F-4s for F/A-18s, but the USMC is also struggling to replace its reconnaissance-dedicated Phantoms.

The F-4G Wild Weasels of the 35th and 52nd Tactical Fighter Wings were one of the big successes of the Gulf War. Armed with High-speed Anti-Radiation Missiles (HARM), they devastated the Iraqi air defence network and reduced enemy missile activity to negligible levels in the space of a few hours, thanks to the APR-47 Radar Homing and Warning System. This system enables Wild Weasel crews to instantly locate enemy radars when they start operating and pass their signatures straight into the HARM's electronic guidance system. Wild Weasels armed with four HARMs apiece accompanied most Coalition strike packages into Iraq and it is claimed that only one Coalition aircraft was shot down by a radar-guided SAM while Wild Weasels were present. The 48 F-4Gs based at Sheikh Isa, on Bahrain, flew some 2,500 combat hours during the war and fired over 1,000 HARMs. Only one F-4G was lost, due to problems during an air-to-air refuelling. Also based at Sheikh Isa were 18 RF-4C photo reconnaissance Phantom IIs of the 67th tactical Reconnaissance Wing (TRW) and the Nevada Air National Guard's 192nd Tactical Reconnaissance Squadron. Like their counterparts from the 26th TRW flying out of Incirlik, in Turkey, the Bahrain-based RF-4C crews were much in demand, but the fast-moving battlefield meant much of the intelligence data they collected was out-of-date by the time it was passed up the chain of command to strike units.

For financial reasons the USAF plans to retire all its F-4Gs and RF-4Cs from frontline service by 1993 and pass them on to the Air National Guard. However, there is some concern that there are no replacements available for these highly capable specialist aircraft, with Wild Weasel and reconnaissance versions of the F-16s and F-15E only existing on the drawing board.

Israeli Phantom IIs continue to be used in strike missions over Lebanon. In 1989 Israeli Aircraft Industries began a programme, called *Kurnass 2000*, to upgrade their F-4's avionics, cockpit, radar, structure and maintainability.

Other Phantom users, such as the UK, Spain and Germany, are making plans to replace their F-4s with the new European Fighter Aircraft, but defence cuts mean that examples will remain in service for many years. The Luftwaffe's Phantoms have recently lost their attack role and been moved over to air defence duties covering all of their newly re-unified country.

Users
Germany, Greece, Iran, Israel, Japan, South Korea, Spain, Turkey, UK, USA

Below: A HARM-carrying F-4G turns in for an attack run.

McDonnell Douglas
F-15E Strike Eagle

Type: Two-seat multi-role aircraft, optimised for all-weather/night air-to-air and deep interdiction missions.

A recent pool of USAF pilots voted the Strike Eagle as the aircraft "they most wanted to fly". The result is not surprising given the F-15E's tremendous performance, warload and night attack systems. Pilots say it combines the strike power of the F-111 with the power and manoeuvreability of the F-15C Eagle fighter.

The Strike Eagle project started as a result of USAF efforts in the early 1980s to develop a dual-role fighter to replace its ageing F-4E Phantom IIs and augment its F-111 interdiction force. Modified versions of the F-15 air superiority fighter proved more successful in tests in 1983 than F-16 variants. It took three years for the first of three prototypes to fly but the result has certainly been worth the wait.

Externally, the F-15E is similar to a two-seat F-15A/D — except for the

Dimensions	F-15C	F-15C Fast	F-15E
Length (ft/m)	63.75/19.43	63.75/19.43	63.75/19.43
Span (ft/m)	42.81/13.05	42.81/13.05	42.81/13.05
Height (ft/m)	18.46/5.63	18.46/5.63	18.46/5.63
Wing area (ft²/m²)	608/56.50	608/56.50	608/5.50
Aspect ratio	3.01	3.01	3.01

Weights			
Empty (lb/kg)	29.180/13,236	30,300/13,700	32,000/14,515
Clean takeoff (lb/kg)	44,500/20,815	55,270/25,070	56,970/25,842
Max takeoff (lb/kg)	68,000/30,844	68,000/30,844	81,000/36,742
Max external load (lb/kg)	16,000/7,258	12,730/5,774	24,000/10,885
Hardpoint	9	9	18

Power			
	2 x F-100-PW-200 tfx	2 F100-PW-200 tf	2 x F-100-PW-200 tf
Max (lb st/kN)	25,000/111.0	25,000/111.0	25,000/111.0
Mil (lb st/kN)	16,200/72.0	16,200/72.0	16,200/72.0

Fuel			
Internal (lb/kg)	13,455/6,103	23,205/10,526	23,205/10,526
External (lb/kg)	11,700/5,310	11,700/5,310	N/A
Fraction	0.30	0.42	0.41

Loadings			
Max thrust	1.12 – 0.74	0.90 – 0.74	0.88 – 0.62
Mil thrust	0.73 – 0.48	0.59 – 0.48	0.56 – 0.40
Wing clean to (lb/ft²/kg/m²)	73/357	91/444	94/457
Wing max to (lb/ft²/kg/m²)	112/546	112/546	133/650

Performance			
Vmax hi	M = 2.5	N/A	N/A
Vmax lo	M = 1.2	N/A	N/A
Ceiling (ft/m)	65,000/19,800	N/A	N/A
Initial climb (ft/min/m/sec)	50,000/254	N/A	N/A
Takeoff roll (ft/m)	900/275	N/A	N/A
Landing roll (ft/m)	N/A	N/A	N/A

First flight	Feb 1979	N/A	Jul 1980 (protoype)

dark grey camouflage scheme — however major changes have been made internally. Central to the F-15E's attack capability are its Hughes APG-70 radar and Low-Altitude Navigation and Targeting Infra-Red by Night (LANTIRN) pods. The high-resolution APG-70 radar allows the Strike Eagle crew to locate targets as small as individual buildings through cloud and at night. The LANTIRN system pods — the navigation pod provides imagery, while the targeting pod contains a laser designator — enable laser-guided munitions to be delivered with pin-point accuracy at night. A terrain following radar system is fitted to allow high-speed/low-level penetration of enemy air space. A permanent feature of the F-15E are conformal fuel tanks (CFTs) which are similar to the Fuel And Sensor Tactical packs carried on by some F-15C/D fighters. The Strike Eagle's CFTs are adapted to carry ordnance tangentially to reduce drag. In total, the F-15E has 18 hardpoints capable of carrying ordnance.

Cockpit arrangements are also very different from other Eagles. The

Below: A development of the F-15D Eagle trainer, the F-15E Strike Eagle is primed for deep-strike interdiction.

Bottom: The brute power from two F100-PW-200 turbofans bestow the F-15E with an impressive turn of speed.

Below: A quartet of the US Air Force's latest and most potent dual-role attack/air superiority fighter, the F-15E Strike Eagle. With a 24,500lb (11,113kg) weapon load, the F-15E can perform long-range, deep-strike missions by day or night.

head-up display can project images from the LANTIRN, so the pilot can fly the plane with the system. The LANTIRN image is also available to the Weapons Systems Operator. A moving-map display is also fitted. The basic flight systems have been modified to make them more user friendly. A new engine bay has been developed to allow the installation of either the General Electric F110 or Pratt & Whitney F100 engine. An impressive war load can be carried, including AIM-7F/M Sparrow, AIM-9J/L/M/N Sidewinder and AIM-120A AMRAAM air-to-air missiles. Air-to-ground armament is equally varied, including AGM-65 Maverick missiles, GBU-10/-12/-24 laser-guided bombs, GBU-15 glide bombs, assorted cluster bomb units and Mk 82/83/84 bombs.

The first operational F-15E unit, the 4th Tactical Fighter Wing's (TFW) 336th Tactical Fighter Squadron (TFS), was formed at the end of 1989 at Seymour-Johnson Air Force Base, in South Carolina, with 24 aircraft. Within months of its formation the squadron was deployed to the Middle East as part of Operation *Desert Shield*.

Its first base was at Thumrait, in Oman, but this proved to be too far away from the Kuwaiti Theatre of Operations (KTO) so the Strike Eagles moved to Al Kharj, in central Saudi Arabia, in December 1990. Back at Seymour-Johnson, the 335th TFS ("The Chiefs") achieved operational status with the Strike Eagle in October 1990. Two months later it was also in Saudi Arabia.

Strike Eagles were in the first wave of Coalition aircraft to strike deep into Iraq in the first hours of the Gulf War. A strike package of 22 F-15Es from the 336th TFS destroyed fixed Scud missile sites near Al Qaim in the opening minutes of *Desert Storm*. Another six F-15Es hit Scud sites near H-2 airfield. These first attacks were carried out with cluster and general-purpose bombs because the LANTIRN targeting pods had yet to arrive in-theatre. During the second week of the war the 335th TFS marked the LANTIRN targeting pod's combat debut when they dropped their first laser-guided bomb. The Strike Eagle's outstanding night attack capability meant they were used almost exclusively for

nocturnal missions, and crews had to learn to put their biological clocks in reverse. Hardened aircraft shelters, bridges, tanks, artillery, communications sites, ammunition dumps and truck convoys all received the attention of the night-flying Strike Eagles. The 335th TFS also claimed to have destroyed an Iraqi McDonnell Douglas 500 helicopter on 14 February 1991 with a laser-guided bomb.

Iraqi attacks on Israel with Scud missiles launched from mobile launcher vehicles similar to articulated trucks provided the Strike Eagle pilots with their greatest challenge. Conventional photo-reconnaissance techniques proved useless at detecting the small missile launchers so some unusual methods had to be adopted to deal with the Iraqi missile threat. Special Forces teams and Boeing E-8 Joint-Surveillance Target Attack Radar System (J-STARS) aircraft were deployed over western Iraq to watch for Scud launches. Formations of Strike Eagles were sent on continuous air patrols over the Scud launch areas armed with GBU-10s, Mk.82 general-purpose bombs and CBU-87 cluster bombs. When missile launches were detected the Strike Eagles were

vectored to the target area and began searches with their APG-70 radar and LANTIRN systems. If the Strike Eagles were fast enough off the mark, they caught the Scud launchers before they could escape back to the safety of their hardened bunkers. No other Coalition aircraft possessed the capability to succeed in this almost impossible mission. Dozens of Scud launchers were destroyed by the Strike Eagles; some missile launches were even spotted by the F-15E crews flying high over western Iraq.

The flexibility of the Strike Eagle was demonstrated after the Gulf War ceasefire when the 4th TFW's aircraft were drafted in to help ease the pressure on the F-15C air defence units by flying combat air patrols over Iraq and Kuwait. By the end of the war the F-15Es had flown more than 2,200 combat sorties and 7,700 combat hours.

Some 45 Iraqi aircraft were destroyed on the ground, 23 radio relay stations knocked out, 36 bridges or pontoons hit, 478 armoured vehicles destroyed and around 80 Scuds taken out. Two Strike Eagles were lost in combat.

After the end of the Gulf War,

Above: Though not carrying any other stores, the nearest of these two 57th FWW F-15Es does sport a LANTIRN pod on a pylon beneath the intake.

Seymour-Johnson AFB became home to the USAF's first Composite Wing (containing more than one type of aircraft), when the 4th TFW was merged with the 68th Air Refuelling Wing to form the 4th Wing. Another Composite Wing is to be formed at Mountain Home AFB in 1992, comprising a F-15E squadron, F-15C squadron, KC-10A tankers, E-3 AWACS and eventually B-52s. During 1993 and 1994, the USAF intends to re-equip the 48th TFW at RAF Lakenheath, UK, with 48 Strike Eagles, in place of the units current inventory of 72 F-111Fs. By early 1992, the USAF boasted some 95 Strike Eagles and had another 57 on order, but continued pressure on the US defence budget has led to uncertainty over whether the USAF will have enough funds to complete its planned F-15E purchases.

User
USA

McDonnell Douglas F/A-18 Hornet

Type: Single-seat twin-engined multi-role carrier- and land-based fighter/attack aircraft; fully combat-capable two seaters are designated F-18B. The designation F/A-18 is often used, but is strictly unofficial. A dedicated reconnaissance variant is under development, while the F-18C and D, equipped with ASPJ and compatible with IIR Maverick and AMRAAM, have entered service.

The F/A-18 Hornet marks a departure from the accepted custom of

designing a fighter to fulfil a single role then adapting it for others, being a dedicated multi-role type from the outset. In the early 1970s the US Navy was in the market for a multi-role fighter to replace both its ageing Phantom fighters and its Corsair attack bombers, and attention was focused on the USAF light fighter competition, which was held in the form of a competitive flyoff between the General Dynamics F-16 and the Northrop F-17. It was widely anticipated that the winner of the contest

Dimensions	F/A-18A
Length (ft/m)	56.00/17.07
Span (ft/m)	37.50/11.43
Height (ft/m)	15.29/4.66
Wing area (sq ft/m²)	400/37.17
Aspect ratio	3.52

Weights	
Empty (lb/kg)	21,830/ 9,900
Clean takeoff (lb/kg)	35,800/16,240
Max takeoff (lb/kg)	51,900/23,540
Max external load (lb/kg)	17,000/ 7,711
Hardpoints	5

Power	2 x F404-GE-400 tf
Max (lb st/kN)	16,000/71.2
Mil (lb st/kN)	10,600/47.2

Fuel	
Internal (lb/kg)	10,860/4,925
External (lb/kg)	7,000/3,175
Fraction	0.30

Loadings	
Max thrust	0.89 – 0.62
Mil thrust	0.59 – 0.41
Wing clean to (lb/sq ft/kg/m²)	90/437
Wing max to (lb/sq ft/kg/m²)	130/634

Performance	
Vmax hi	M = 1.8
Vmax lo	M = 1.01
Ceiling (ft/m)	50,000/15,250
Initial climb (ft/min/m/sec)	50,000/254
Takeoff roll (ft/m)	N/A
Landing roll (ft/m)	N/A

First flight	18 Nov 1982

would be selected, but when the Navy came to review its requirements in detail, its decision was that not only did the Northrop entrant provide extra flight safety in the form of two engines, but it also offered more development potential. The flight safety emphasis reflected the fact that most carrier aircraft flights are over the trackless ocean, whereas Air Force missions are often overland.

McDonnell Douglas, with their vast experience in building carrier fighters, teamed with Northrop for the project, which emerged as the F-18, a rather larger aircraft than the F-17 had been and considerably heavier. It was first intended to produce both fighter and attack variants based on a single airframe while Nor-

throp were to build a lighter and slightly more potent export version called the F-18L for land-based use. This was possible because the F-18L did not have to endure the rigours of carrier operations, with catapult launches and arrested landings.

In the event, McDonnell Douglas produced a tour de force. Drawing on the experience of advanced cockpits they had gained on the F-15, they combined HOTAS with CRT multi-function displays to produce what was in effect a new-generation cockpit, with few old-fashioned dials and tape instruments. Instead there

Below: A USMC F/A-18C Hornet reveals a "sting" including HARM and Harpoon missiles.

Above: Each F/A-18 Hornet has a total of nine weapons stations (two wingtip; six underwing; one centreline) on which a wide range of ordnance, such as the Snakeye retarded bombs visible on these US Navy machines, can be carried.

were three screens on which information could be called up by computer as required by pushing a few buttons, which enabled a single crewman to command the data needed for either the fighter or the attack mission.

In fighter configuration the Hornet carries two Sidewinders on wingtip rails and two Sparrows conformally on the fuselage; for the attack mission the Sidewinders are retained but the Sparrows are replaced by a FLIR pod and a laser designator and target marker pod in about half an hour. The radar is the Hughes APG-65, with numerous high quality air-to-air and air-to-ground modes, including real beam ground-mapping, Doppler beam sharpening sector and patch, terrain avoidance, precision velocity update, and sea surface search, and the comprehensive avionics fit includes RWR, ECM and INS, while computer capacity is almost half as great again as that of the F-15. All in all, the Hornet is a very capable weapon system packaged into an airframe/engine combination which has few equals.

Hornets first saw combat service with the US Navy during the 1986 strike on Libya. The US Navy deployed 106 Hornets on the six carriers that took part in Operation *Desert Storm*, and 84 flew with units of the 3rd Marine Air Wing based on Bahrain. Hornets flew air defence, suppression of enemy air defence, interdiction, close air support, escort, counter-air and anti-shipping missions. F/A-18s from the USS *Saratoga* scored the only US Navy fixed-wing "kills" of the war when they shot down two MiG-21s on 17 January 1991. Royal Canadian Air Force CF-18s also took part in the Gulf War flying almost 1,000 combat missions.

The US Navy places great reliance on the Hornet in its re-equipment plans for the coming decade. Its new F/A-18E/Fs are set to feature new engines, enlarged wing area and extra fuel to enable them to carry out both strike and fleet defence missions. The new Hornet version will have a combat radius of 400nm (741km), carrying either a large bomb load or four

Below: A USMC Hornet in the attack configuration, with FLIR and laser designator pods.

AIM-120 AMRAAMs and two AIM-9 Sidewinders AAMs. A further 238 F/A-18C/Ds are to be produced over the next five years until the new versions becomes available.

In the summer of 1991, the Kuwaiti Air Force became the fifth air arm to take delivery of Hornets, a year late because of the Iraqi invasion.

Users
Australia, Canada, Kuwait, Spain, USA

Above: For the battlefield air interdiction role, the Hornet carries cluster munitions.

Below: The Hornet can carry a heavy bomb load as far as the A-7 Corsair II, but faster.

LTV A-7 Corsair II

Type: Single-seat single-engined carrier- and land-based attack fighter. Variants include two-seat trainers.

From the 1970s through to the mid-1980s, the A-7 Corsair II was the workhorse of the USAF's close air support/battlefield interdiction (CAS/BAI) force and the US Navy's carrier-borne light attack squadrons. It has now been largely superceded by the F/A-18, F-16 and A-10A in frontline US service, but still features strongly in the reserve component.

Like the F-4 Phantom II, the A-7 started life as a US Navy project that was quickly adopted by the USAF when its potential was fully realised. It saw extensive service in Vietnam from US Navy carriers and USAF bases in South Vietnam, with total sorties running to over 100,000.

The definitive US Navy version was the A-7E, while the USAF concentrated on the A-7D which featured very different electronics. In the late 1980s the USAF modified some 80 A-7Ds and A-7Ks (two-seaters) for night attack missions by fitting Forward-Looking Infra Red (FLIR) and automatic terrain following systems. They were delivered from 1987 but current plans call for them to be

Dimensions	A-7D	A-7E
Length (ft/m)	46.13/14.06	46.13/14.06
Span (ft/m)	38.73/11.80	38.73/11.80
Height (ft/m)	16.13/4.92	16.13/4.92
Wing area (sq ft/m²)	375/34.85	375/34.85
Aspect ratio	4.0	4.0

Weights		
Empty (lb/kg)	19,781/8,975	18,800/8,530
Clean takeoff (lb/kg)	30,000/13,608	29,000/13,155
Max takeoff (lb/kg)	42,000/19,050	42,000/19,050
Max external load (lb/kg)	15,000/6,800	15,000/6,800
Hardpoints	6	6

Power		
	1 x TF41-A-1 tf	1 x TF41-A-2 tf
Max (lb st/kN)	N/A	N/A
Mil (lb st/kN)	14,250/63.3	15,000/66.7

Fuel		
Internal (lb/kg)	9,600/4,355	9,600/4,355
External (lb/kg)	7,800/3,540	7,800/3,540
Fraction	0.32	0.33

Loadings		
Max thrust	N/A	N/A
Mil thrust	0.48−0.34	0.50−0.36
Wing clean to (lb/sq ft/kg/m²)	80/390	77/377
Wing max to (lb/sq ft/kg/m²)	112/547	112/547

Performance		
Vmax hi	N/A	N/A
Vmax lo	M = 0.92	M = 0.92
Ceiling (ft/m)	42,000/12,800	42,000/12,800
Initial climb (ft/min/m/sec)	15,000/76	15,000/76
Takeoff roll (ft/m)	< 4,000/1,200	<4,000/1,200
Landing roll (ft/m)	N/A	N/A

First flight	Sep 1968	N/A

replaced by F-16A/Bs by 1993. Corsair IIs from the Ohio Air National Guard gave the A-7D what will probably be its last combat outing in USAF service in December 1989, when they flew close air support missions over Panama.

The US Navy began to gradually phase out its A-7s in the mid-1980s when the first F/A-18 Hornets entered service. Corsair IIs supported Operation *Urgent Fury* in Grenada and an A-7 from the USS *Independence* was lost to Syrian anti-aircraft fire over Lebanon in 1983. A-7Es were also heavily involved in strikes against Iranian naval forces during the so-called "Tanker War" in 1987-88. In 1990 the A-7E squadrons (VA-46 and 72) on the USS *John F. Kennedy* were in the process of converting to the Hornet when Iraq invaded Kuwait. During Operation *Desert Storm* the 24 A-7Es flew 731 combat sorties and 3,100 combat hours. They flew strike missions against Iraq with conventional and cluster bombs. In spite of their age, they performed remarkably well and were easier to maintain and launch from catapults than more modern naval attack aircraft.

Export versions continue to serve in the Greek (A-7H) and Portuguese (A-7P) Air Forces.

Users
Greece, Portugal, USA

Below: A two-seat A-7K leads a single-seat A-7D.

Combat Tactics

T HE task of the attack aircraft can be defined as to hit the target swiftly and accurately with whatever munitions are carried, and return safely to base. That is not to imply that avoiding losses is the major factor — war is war, and losses will occur — but keeping the attrition level within tolerable limits remains one of the priorities. To carry out the task as stated three conditions must be satisfied: the enemy defences must be penetrated, both outbound and on the return leg; the target must be located and correctly identified; and aiming has to be accurate.

Methods of penetrating enemy defences vary according to the strength and sophistication of the hostile detection, reporting, command and control network, and how much intelligence is available about its capabilities. The usual worst case yardstick is generally held to be an all-out conventional war in central Europe, but it should be remembered that the central European scenario is, barring grave political miscalculations, an unlikely one, while limited wars in other parts of the globe occur quite frequently.

No country in the world can muster a comprehensive, multi-layered air defence. There will always be strong points, usually centred on key features such as airfields, ground radars and command posts, while communications bottlenecks such as bridges and roads through constricting geographical features will normally have better than average defences against air attack. By the same token, there will be areas where the counter-air assets are spread thinly, and where there are gaps or shadows in the radar coverage. Careful planning can route the attack force around the strongly defended areas wherever possible and make the best use of deceptive measures, including flight paths chosen to keep the enemy guessing as to the identify of the actual target until the last possible moment, though radical changes of course will make fuel state more critical and in-

Route planning

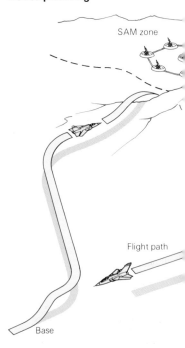

SAM zone

Flight path

Base

Below: Peacetime safety and noise rules prevent these bomb-armed RAF Tornados from flying at operational heights.

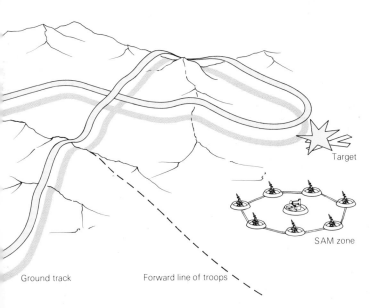

Target

SAM zone

Ground track

Forward line of troops

In a typical low-level strike mission aircrew will attempt to use terrain features to conceal their approach to the target and their return flight to base. The SAM site near the target is thus partially countered, but the more distant site is still a threat.

crease the time spent at risk over hostile territory. Mission planning will also involve striking a balance between fuel and munitions in determining the load to be carried.

The mission profile chosen for a specific strike is an important factor. At high altitudes either maximum speed or fuel economy at cruise speeds will be improved, but the distance at which the aircraft can be detected by radar will be increased, alerting the defences earlier and, unless the altitude is extreme, the aircraft will find itself in the optimum engagement envelope of many long-range surface-to-air missiles. Nor does high altitude make for precision attack.

Medium altitude is often a reasonable compromise, offering good fuel economy and endurance while placing the aircraft above the effective reach of many surface-to-air systems, and while detection distance is still far too great for comfort medium altitude does permit accurate target location via ground mapping radar, especially using Doppler beam sharpening, and an accurate diving attack.

Low-altitude penetration also has both advantages and disadvantages:

it can sometimes avoid detection altogether, while exposure time is measured in seconds, often too few for defensive systems to track and fire. On the other hand, it compounds the difficulties of navigation and target location, accurate aiming becomes a problem, and without special equipment the mission cannot be flown at night or in adverse weather. Finally it is heavy on fuel and restricts range.

The accent is currently on low-level penetration, but medium and high level can be used in some circumstances: high-altitude, high-speed penetration is really the province of the strategic bomber armed with long-range stand-off missiles, but tactical penetration can be made where the defences are weak with the

Above right: The original A-10 mission would have involved a version of World War II cab-rank tactics, with loitering Thunderbolts ready to support ground forces as required.

Right: Revised tactics to deal with intense air defences emphasise sea-level penetration, smart weapons and ECM.

Breda Twin 40L70 aircraft engagement

As attack aircraft have been forced lower, air defences have adapted to the threat: with modern fire control and proximity-fuzed ammunition, Breda calculate that even a supersonic attack could expect to sustain hits by 3,578 splinters in this scenario, with two Twin 40L70 guns defending.

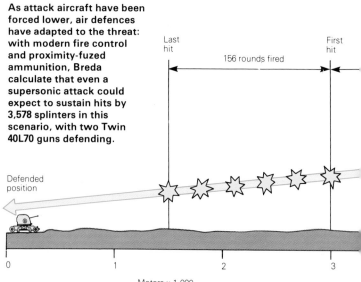

A-10 designed CAS mission

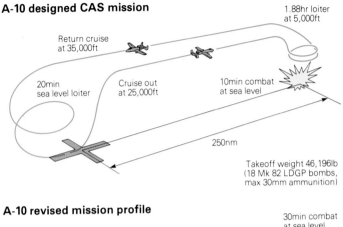

1.88hr loiter
at 5,000ft

Return cruise
at 35,000ft

20min
sea level loiter

Cruise out
at 25,000ft

10min combat
at sea level

250nm

Takeoff weight 46,196lb
(18 Mk 82 LDGP bombs,
max 30mm ammunition)

A-10 revised mission profile

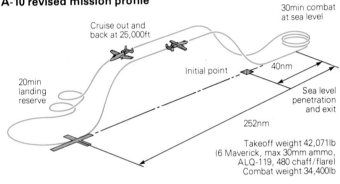

30min combat
at sea level

Cruise out and
back at 25,000ft

Initial point

40nm

20min
landing
reserve

Sea level
penetration
and exit

252nm

Takeoff weight 42,071lb
(6 Maverick, max 30mm ammo,
ALQ-119, 480 chaff/flare)
Combat weight 34,400lb

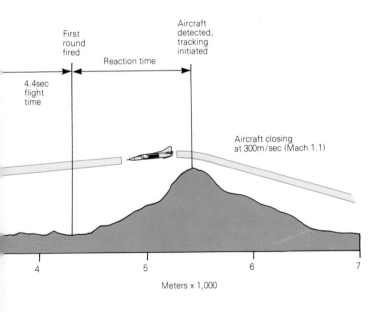

First
round
fired

Aircraft
detected,
tracking
initiated

Reaction time

4.4sec
flight
time

Aircraft closing
at 300m/sec (Mach 1.1)

4   5   6   7

Meters x 1,000

help of active and passive counter-measures and the weapons launched before the full strength of the defences is encountered. While this form of attack can be used against land targets, it can be particularly effective at sea — in a mass attack on a carrier task force, for example.

Medium-altitude penetration relies heavily on countermeasures and defence suppression, and while it is effective against moderate defences doubts are often expressed about its validity in a modern war zone. In 1983 a US carrier task force launched a strike on Lebanon and lost two aircraft, an Intruder and a Corsair. Given the current preoccupation with ultra low level penetration, ground defences are also concentrating on this area, possibly to the detriment of other defence levels, but it must be said that medium-altitude penetration against anything other than the weakest defences would require a great back-up effort, involving Wild Weasel defence suppression aircraft and specialised electronic warfare aircraft such as the EA-6 Prowler and EF-111 Raven, plus fighters carrying out sweeps and flying barrier patrols.

At ultra low level the attack aircraft flies in an invisible corridor with well defined boundaries set by altitude, speed and flight capability. The corridor tends to vary for different aircraft, depending on their gust response and whether they have specialised low-flying avionics. Low-flying systems are of the greatest importance: air defence systems vary in effectiveness, but the ground always rates 100%.

Where possible the mission profile will normally be hi-lo-lo-hi, with a high-altitude approach over friendly territory at an economical cruising speed followed by a descent to low level for a rapid subsonic penetration. The homeward leg will be the reverse, though if enemy fighters are encountered and fuel permits the low-level egress will be supersonic. Such a procedure can be damaging to the enemy in its own right: tests have shown that an aircraft at low level and supersonic speed sets up a shock wave than can damage sensitive electronic equipment, overturn soft vehicles and cause hearing impairment to troops.

Navigation is the next problem. The most basic method is to designate the target in a grid square and fly there by a direct route using map, compass, stop watch and a great deal of mental agility.

This method works in clear weather against unsophisticated defences where only a shallow penetration is needed, but it will be rare for all three conditions to be met, and modern attack fighters are equipped with nav/attack systems of varying degrees of sophistication. Ideally, the route should be carefully planned beforehand to delay detection for as long as possible, to avoid defen-

Tornado lo-lo-lo-lo mission

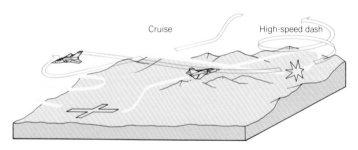

Cruise

High-speed dash

Above: The Tornado is capable of missions of 500nm or more radius with a typical weapons load without flying higher than 200ft. The bulk of the mission is flown at cruising speed, **followed by a high-speed dash over the target: the point at which the dash will be initiated will be determined by estimates of the defences likely to be encountered.**

Low-level strike corridor

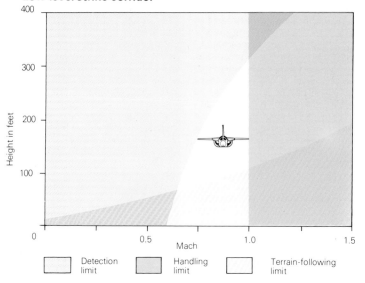

Detection limit   Handling limit   Terrain-following limit

sive strongpoints, to confuse the defenders as to intent and, finally, to give the best possible line of approach to the target combined with the most suitable heading for the bug-out.

The pilot's workload is high. He has to fly the aeroplane accurately at low level, keeping a sharp lookout for obstacles ahead, enemy fighters behind and SAMs anywhere while staying on course, identifying turning points and making adjustments to fly around patches of weather if he is not

Above: The parameters of the attack corridor will vary, but at low levels Mach 1 will be a practical limit, leaving a balance to be struck between keeping clear of terrain and staying hidden from radar.

equipped to go through them. This is where a good nav/attack system really comes into its own. At its most basic it will include an inertial navigation system (INS) preset to the known position on the ground before

Tornado hi-lo-lo-hi mission

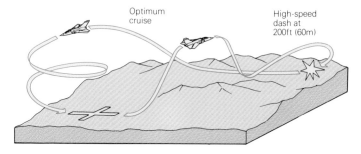

Optimum cruise

High-speed dash at 200ft (60m)

Above: If it is possible to fly the outward and return legs of the mission at optimum cruise altitude the Tornado's mission radius rises to more than 850nm, even allowing for the high-speed

penetration dash to and from the target which is unlikely to be less than 100nm. The weapons load is not specified, but would certainly include ECM pods as well as offensive stores.

take off and able to maintain a high degree of accuracy during the mission — no more than a couple of miles' error per hour.

A Doppler can add to the accuracy by feeding an accurate speed over the ground into the computer since ground speed differs from air speed as shown on the ASI according to wind speed and direction and barometric pressure variation. A moving map display as used in the Harrier gives a continually updated position over the ground; otherwise the information is generally given in terms of coordinates on either head-up or head-down displays. Waypoints can be stored in the computer, which tells the pilot when and how much to turn. A head-up display is invaluable, as when a pilot is flying manually at low level looking down inside the cockpit is to be avoided if possible, although head-down displays are generally located at the top of the dash, where they are within the pilot's peripheral vision.

War does not stop at sunset, and darkness and adverse visibility degrade optically laid counter-air weapons, while cloud, rain and fog reduce the effectiveness of infra-red homing missiles quite dramatically. That helps attack aircraft penetrate the defences unscathed, but it compounds the difficulties of navigating accurately to the target, and a more sophisticated avionics fit is needed, often with a second crew member to share the workload. The increased capacity of a two-man crew also allows a more capable countermeasures suite to be included.

The first priority is to allow the aircraft to fly the same low-level mission as it would in daylight, which means avoiding contact with the ground, and three main systems exist, with varying capabilities. Forward-looking infra red (flir) pierces the darkness and presents a TV-quality picture on a screen in the cockpit, allowing the pilot to fly much as he would in

F/A-18 radar attack

Above right: A prominent navaid in the Harrier's cockpit is the Ferranti moving map display.

Right: High-resolution radar mapping is the key to the Hornet's attack capability.

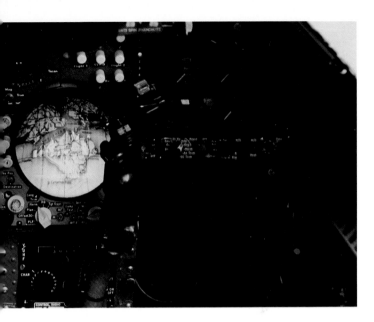

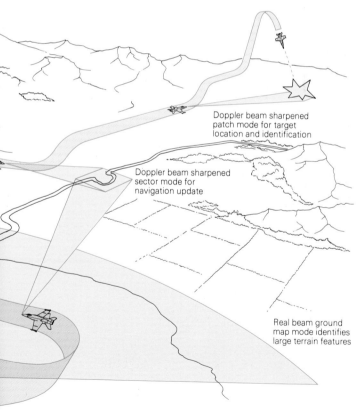

Doppler beam sharpened
patch mode for target
location and identification

Doppler beam sharpened
sector mode for
navigation update

Real beam ground
map mode identifies
large terrain features

Right: Hornet Flir image. Infrared is most useful for targeting in the final stages of an attack.

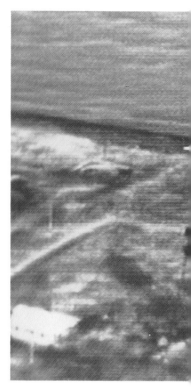

daylight, although of course the field of view (FOV) is far more limited. Flir gives a night capability, but its adverse weather capability is strictly limited, and as it is in service at the moment, Flir is more used for night attack than penetrating the target. Currently under development is Lantirn (Low-altitude navigation and targeting by infra-red at night), which will give a round-the-clock capability to the F-16, A-10 and other aircraft.

Next comes terrain-avoidance radar, whose elongated oval-section radar scan in front of the aircraft combines with a computer-generated template to warn of rising ground ahead and flash flightpath commands onto a screen. Various clearance levels can be preset — 250ft (76m), 500ft (152m) or 1,000ft (305m) are usual, or intermediate settings can be used if desirable. The system does not prevent the pilot from flying into the ground; it simply gives him the information necessary to avoid it.

Finally there is terrain-following radar, which, linked to the autopilot, actually flies the aircraft close to a preset height over the ground. Again, various clearance levels can be selected, normally between 200ft (60m) and 1,000ft (305m), and it is also possible for various grades of ride to be selected, normally hard, medium or soft. Hard ride keeps the aeroplane closest to the selected altitude, but at a considerable cost in crew comfort, and would normally only be selected to traverse heavily defended areas. Other settings are selected according to the threat. The transition to automatic terrain following mode does not mean that the pilot sits with nothing to do: apart from monitoring navigation functions, fuel states and so on he keeps a watchful eye on the TF radar presentation to ensure that it is working correctly.

On a deep penetration mission the navigation system needs to be updated at intervals to obtain the degree of accuracy necessary for a first-pass blind strike to be made. On the flight plan, which is often stored on a cassette tape and fed into the com-

Tornado terrain following

Terrain-following radar generates a theoretical ski-toe shaped envelope projected forward of the aircraft, and compares this with the profile of the terrain ahead. In the case of Tornado, penetration of the envelope by the terrain generates an automatic climb command which is passed to the autopilot and flight-director computers, resulting in an input to the control surfaces, and to the pilot's head-up and head-down displays, as shown here.

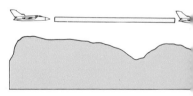

2151

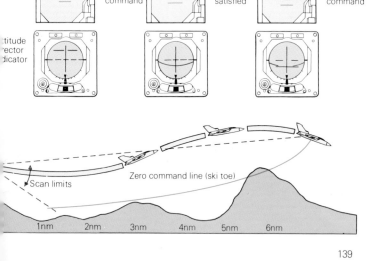

-scope splay	Ground returns penetrate ski toe	Ground returns on ski toe	Ground returns below ski toe
HUD	Pull-up command	Command satisfied	Push-over command
-titude -rector dicator			

Scan limits

Zero command line (ski toe)

1nm   2nm   3nm   4nm   5nm   6nm

puter in the cockpit, various radar-reflective or radar-significant points will have been stored, and as these points are approached — not necessarily too closely — a few sweeps are made with the radar and their exact position established. This information is fed into the computer, which then updates the actual aircraft position, giving a very high degree of accuracy.

The final avionics aids to penetration are countermeasures, which are both active and passive. Radar warning receivers, (RWRs) of varying degrees of complexity are becoming standard on attack aircraft: they detect when the aircraft is being painted by radar, and at the most basic level give an aural warning with a visual indication of which quadrant the hostile emission is coming from. At the top end of the market they not only detect a multiplicity of emissions but also classify them according to their nature — search, SAM, air-to-air or whatever — with a fairly accurate assessment of bearing, range, function and whether or not they constitute a threat, all of which is displayed in the cockpit, though in very intensive areas only those considered to be the greatest threat will be indicated. RWRs may even be able to take direct action in the form of jamming without the intervention of a crew member, although they can always be overridden at need. A typical example would be a low and fast aircraft acquired by radar in a position where it would be able to shake off detection by using terrain masking, in which case active jamming, being an emission, might continue to betray its position.

Jamming can consist of expendables in the form of flares or chaff, or active noise or deception jamming. ECM pods can be carried, although pods sterilise pylons that could otherwise be used for something more offensive, or an ECM suite can be fitted internally. ECM suites tend to be very comprehensive, and are designed to be flexible in countering new threats through programmability. Software

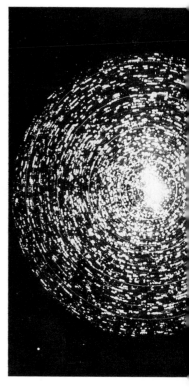

Inverse gain deception jamming

Deception jamming involves the transmission of fake return signals which the victim will accept as genuine. These are

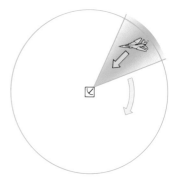

Normal operation: the antenna is pointing at the target aircraft, which returns a genuine echo seen on the PPI (left) as a target

often sent when the antenna of the victim is not directly facing the jammer, so they must be very powerful in order to leak into the antenna via a sidelobe. The fake pulse will then be of an appropriate strength to be accepted as genuine.

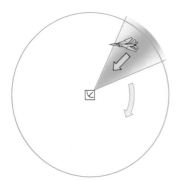

With the aircraft on the edge of the beam, the radar will reject the true target in favour of a powerful fake echo apparently on another bearing

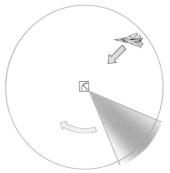

By transmitting a massive fake echo later in the scan pattern, the jammer can create another target on a totally false bearing

141

can be altered to meet a changing threat far more easily and cheaply than hardware, the main difficulty being deciding at what command level the authority to initiate a change should be vested, which is of course a wartime problem; in peacetime speed is not of the essence.

Having successfully penetrated the air defence system, it is vital for the attacker to locate the target in time for a first-pass attack; second time around is simply not good enough, as an abortive first pass will only alert the defenders. Another factor is fuel; in many cases there will be insufficient for feints or other deceptive measures if the first pass fails.

At the most basic level, target acquisition will be visual, while successive steps of sophistication lead up through electro-optical means such as flir or televisual acquisition, ground-mapping radar and offset blind bombing to the use of synthetic aperture radar. For all practical purposes there are two main types of targets, those in known locations and those that are mobile; while the latter may be expected to be in a certain area, their exact location is not known. There will also be occasions when previously undetected targets will be discovered.

Visual detection is dependent on daylight and clear weather. Even then a fast jet at low level stands little chance of visually acquiring anything other than a large area target unless it appears fortuitously straight ahead. Normal visual acquisition depends on

the aircraft leaving the shelter of the ground briefly for a pop-up to have a quick look round. The tactical wisdom of such a manoeuvre will depend on the strength of the defences in the specific area; in some cases it will be feasible, in others suicidal.

Flir presents a picture on the screen made up from heat imagery; ideally this is displayed at the exact size that the pilot would see visually, while the focus can be adjusted if required to give a close-up view. The picture is in black and white, and definition in clear air is very good, turning night into day, although only along the line of sight. While generally reckoned to give a night attack capability, flir can also be used to penetrate smoke and dust over the battlefield.

Televisual aids can also be used, as with Maverick; the camera in the nose of the missile displays a picture in the cockpit which the pilot uses to lock on the missile using brightness contrast (light against dark or vice versa). Unfortunately, a high level of contrast is needed, which calls for clear weather and means the direction of attack needs to take the angle of the sun into account to give the greatest amount of contrast. That is why the latest version of Maverick uses IIR for homing and contrast.

Ground-mapping radar is used to scan the terrain ahead and present a picture in the cockpit from which

Below: An airfield target several miles ahead as shown on the radar display of a Tornado.

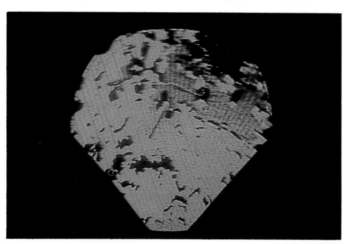

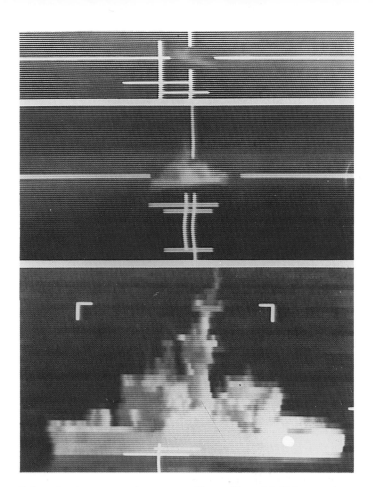

Below: At closer range the target is marked using the hand controller ready for an attack.

Above: Maverick IR image of a US destroyer at acquisition, visual and terminal ranges.

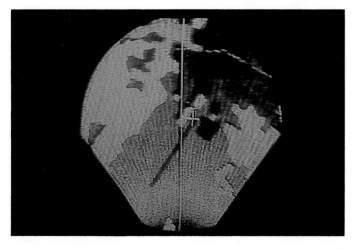

targets may be identified. As slant look angles cause a fair amount of distortion, a computer is used to process the returns and present the picture in plan view, so that it is more easily identified.

Blind bombing is carried out by approaching an easily identifiable point, visually or by radar, at a precomputed speed, altitude, and heading. Once there, the aircraft is pulled into a climb, typically of 30°, and the bombs are released, after which they travel on under their own momentum for about three miles (5km), reaching an altitude of about 3,000ft (914m) en route. This method allows full use of terrain masking to be made. Once the bombs have been released the aircraft is free to reverse course and return to low level.

If no suitable identifiable point exists close to the target an offset point can be used, with a radar return from it fed into the attack computer to give a very accurate position for the aircraft. This form of bombing is exploited even more by using the Rockwell GBU-15, which can be launched as described, the target being acquired via either a television camera or an IIR seeker while the weapon is in flight and lock-on being made by data link.

Synthetic aperture radar (SAR) was first developed for reconnaissance purposes back in the 1960s, but since then advances in processing have allowed the definition to be improved to the level of low-grade photography, an improvement not only good enough to give targeting data, but also one which can be used to detect, and often identify, previously unknown targets to one side or the other of the flight path.

Guided weapons excepted, the accurate release of air-to-ground munitions is beset with difficulties. Bomb or rocket ballistics, aircraft speed, which may reach 900ft (275m) per second, aircraft velocity vector, weapon release parameters, range and even cross-winds all affect the aiming equation, which with modern equipment is taken care of by the stores management and weapons aiming systems. Obviously, the precise moment of weapon release is critical, and a split second delay on

the part of the human operator could cause a gross error, so with many weapons release is also automated.

Irrespective of whether the attack mode is lay-down, toss bombing, low angle dive bombing or dive-toss, the

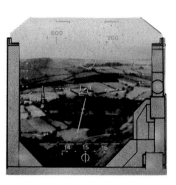

Above: Tornado HUD symbology for a straight-pass attack using an offset aiming point in automatic terrain-following mode.

Below: Offset aiming is used where a target is unlikely to show up clearly on radar. When planning the sortie the crew select a nearby radar-prominent feature — in this case a pylon — and load its coordinates into the nav/attack system along with those of the target.

Offset bomb-aiming

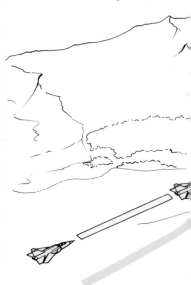

Synthetic aperture radar

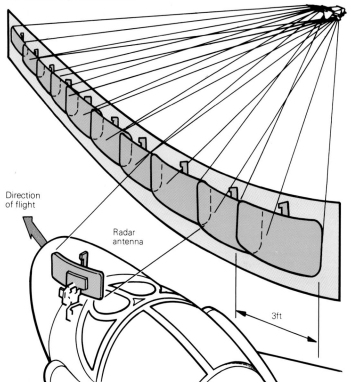

Direction of flight

Radar antenna

3ft

Above: Synthetic aperture radar involves collating a series of returns and analysing differing return angles on left and right halves of the antenna to give a target's relative position.

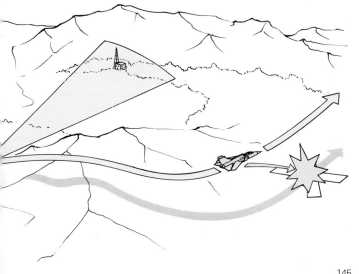

data is fed into the computer beforehand, any time between the mission planning stage and the approach, depending on the weapons and the target. As the attack is commenced the bomb release button is depressed, a process known as pickling, and the bombs will be released when the electrons think they have solved the problem, or when a preset range has been reached. The crew's task is thus simplified; having fed the required data into the number cruncher, all they have to do is to arm the system at the right time, by means of the pickle button, then fly the aircraft accurately towards or over the target.

Two acronyms that occur often in the weapons aiming context are CCIP and CCRP, along with their derivatives CCIP/IP and CCRP/IP.

CCIP stands for continuous computation of impact point, sometimes irreverently known as the death dot, while CCRP is continuous computation of release point. IP stands for initial point.

When flying low over the battlefield or the target area, a weapon released at a given moment will impact at a given spot. The CCIP is that spot, and can be switched on ready for the possibility of a target appearing under the aircraft's flightpath. This instantly available aim point makes a preselected weapon immediately ready for use. With CCIP/IP, the coordinates of a known

Right: An F/A-18 lets go a pair of Mk 82 slicks in a medium-altitude shallow diving attack.

Direct delivery bombing

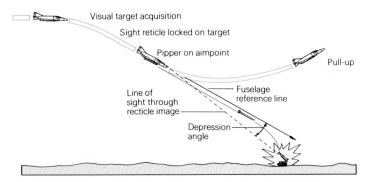

Visual target acquisition
Sight reticle locked on target
Pipper on aimpoint
Pull-up
Line of sight through recticle image
Fuselage reference line
Depression angle

Above: Direct delivery mode is used only as a last resort when a faulty INS has fed incorrect data to the weapons release computer; weapons are released on pickle.

Below: Dive-toss mode gives improved accuracy and allows for evasive manoeuvres during the approach: with the pipper on target, release is automatic.

Dive-toss bombing

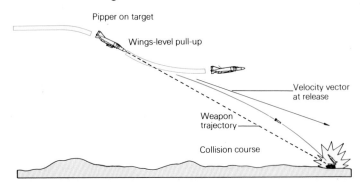

Pipper on target
Wings-level pull-up
Velocity vector at release
Weapon trajectory
Collision course

Dive-glide bombing

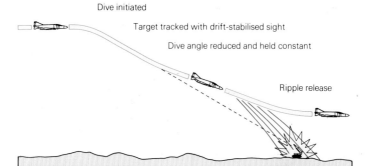

Dive initiated

Target tracked with drift-stabilised sight

Dive angle reduced and held constant

Ripple release

Above: Dive-glide release is used against area targets. The pilot hits the pickle button when the pipper is on target, and the computer carries out the release.

Below: Dive-level or lay-down bombing is used with low-drag weapons and involves the pilot maintaining a constant ground track through the target.

Dive-level bombing

Visual target acquisition

Push-over while tracking target

Initiate pull-up to level approach

point — the initial point — are stored in the nav/attack system before takeoff, together with its relationship to 'the target: once the IP is reached and designated piloting information is displayed, probably on the HUD, which enables the pilot to fly accurately to the target, and the weapon is released automatically at the appropriate moment. The CCIP is adjusted automatically for height, speed and weapon selected, including guns.

CCRP is similar but is used for toss of loft bombing; once the target has been designated weapon release is automatic. CCRP/IP also incorporates an IP which works in exactly the same way as the CCIP/IP: piloting instructions are given in similar fashion and weapons release is again automatic. The degree of automation in both CCIP and CCRP removes one potential cause of aiming error.

The missions that the attack aircraft will be called on to fly vary between close air support and long range interdiction, or possibly anti-shipping sorties. All have their various requirements and tactical approaches.

Close air support/battlefield air interdiction involves shallower penetration of hostile airspace than any other mission. In this scenario targets are frequently in close proximity to friendly forces, and identification is made difficult by smoke and dust, without the additional complication of poor visibility. For conventional fast jets, including armed trainers, target acquisition and identification becomes a major problem. Ideally they would be assisted by a forward air controller (FAC), based either on the ground or in a helicopter, who would allocate targets and direct attacks. The FAC might be in touch with, or even directing, a laser designation team, which would ease the difficulties somewhat; the target would be picked up by the laser kit in the nose of the aircraft and attacked without even being seen. Ideally the attack run would be made from behind the FLOT, the weapons delivered and a prompt egress initiated. Aircraft would operate in two-ship elements as a basic fighting formation, and with luck many

friendly aircraft would be in the area at one time to confuse and saturate the defences. The first priority in this mission would be to knock out hostile ground-based air defence systems, mobile radars and AA guns; the CAS aircraft could then set about enemy armour and APCs.

The A-10 Thunderbolt is the only modern aircraft known to have been designed as a tank-killer. One of the difficulties of air action close to the FLOT is that the enemy forces are deployed, presenting widely spaced targets which are not very suitable for attack by anything other than precision weapons. A fast jet stands little chance of knocking out a single tank unless its flight path takes it almost straight overhead, and even then there is little time to select a weapon and aim. The A-10, by contrast, may be classed as a slow jet, relying on armour and redundant systems to survive hits rather than speed to avoid hits in the first place. Its relatively low speed confers many benefits, reducing the radius of turn to allow the aircraft to remain over one portion of the battlefield with ease and stay below a low cloud base, giving the pilot more time for positive identification and permitting

Pave Penny attack scenario

Above: Ground-based laser designation can be of great help to a pilot carrying out a close-support mission. This is the Ferranti Battlefield Operations Laser Designator used by British troops to designate targets for laser-guided bombs during the Falklands War of 1982.

Below: The AAS-38 Pave Penny pod, standard equipment on the A-10, is able to acquire targets designated by laser-equipped forward air controllers. The pod detects the reflected radiation and indicates the target on the pilot's HUD, enabling the pilot to manoeuvre for an attack.

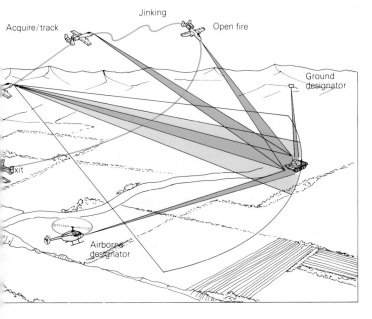

Jinking

Acquire/track

Open fire

Ground designator

Exit

Airborne designator

him to fly really close to the ground and use terrain masking.

The A-10 carries precision weapons — AGM-65 Maverick, which is a launch-and-leave weapon, and the giant GAU-8/A Avenger gun, with its depleted uranium-cored shells. Approaching from behind friendly lines at low level, it pops up briefly to around 700ft (210m), acquires a target, locks on a Maverick, launches and dives away, turning as it does so. The same procedure is followed with the gun, except that the range is rather shorter. The one thing the A-10 is not intended to do is penetrate hostile airspace; if it goes more than 2nm (3.75km) over, it has gone too far.

Behind the battlefield is the interdiction zone. A modern battle is heavily dependent on fuel, munitions and reinforcements, and the battle zone can be roughly defined by the range of modern artillery — within about 15nm (28km) of hostile positions land forces can reasonably be assumed to be deployed, and it is behind this area that the juiciest targets are to be found. Speed of movement, as reinforcements are hurried forward, will dictate that

A-10 low-level gun attack

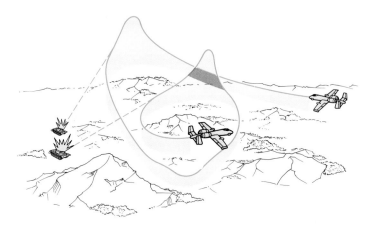

Above: The A-10 spends most of its time less than 100ft (30m) above the ground, popping up briefly to a maximum of 500ft to deliver short bursts of fire.

Below: Terrain masking and three-dimensional evasive jinking are also employed in the run-up to a Maverick launch from 500ft.

A-10 low-level Maverick delivery

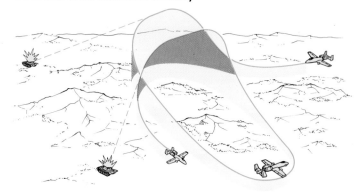

roads are heavily used; roads have to cross rivers and wind through defiles, which constitute choke points. Further back railways will be attacked, and particularly marshalling yards. Once a target is located, it will be hit in force by a dozen or more aircraft, probably using area weapons such as cluster bombs. Harriers, with their forward basing and rapid reaction times, would be used against area targets just behind the deployment zone, while Jaguars, F-16s and Mirages hit targets further back. Still deeper in, Tornados and F-111s would strike at communications,

although they are at first more likely to fight the counter-air battle by strikes against airfields.

If there is any choice, the deep penetration missions will be flown at night or in adverse weather to hamper the defences. Airfields are heavily defended targets and the use of laydown weapons, which involve overflight, has been heavily criticised in some quarters, but while stand-off weapons may be preferable from some viewpoints, the attacking aircraft has to pull up to acquire the target and lock on before release, which makes it vulnerable. An alter-

ZSU-23-4 avoidance tactics

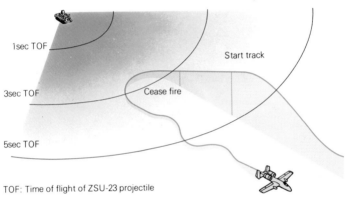

3sec linear flight path from start track to cease fire; open fire after 1.5sec

1sec TOF

Start track

3sec TOF

Cease fire

5sec TOF

TOF: Time of flight of ZSU-23 projectile

Above: At GAU-8/A range an A-10 can deliver a 1.5sec burst and be back under a Shilka's minimum elevation before the 23mm projectiles can reach it.

Below: The A-10 should be able to return to terrain masking after the attack in less time than it takes the SA-8 to acquire, lock on and launch.

SA-8 avoidance tactics

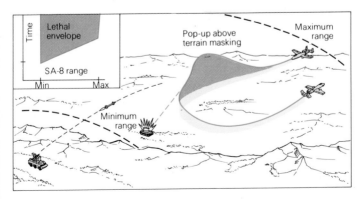

Time

Lethal envelope

SA-8 range

Min   Max

Pop-up above terrain masking

Maximum range

Minimum range

native view is that if a minimum of eight aircraft are sent to attack an airfield, with two or four toss-bombing with conventional bombs set to airburst in order to keep the defenders' heads down while the others run in from different directions and in rapid succession with laydown weapons, casualties should be light.

Successful attacks on bridges and other small, hard targets demand pinpoint accuracy. Night attacks are preferred, not only for defensive purposes but also because the majority of enemy movement will take place at night: a bridge dropped early in the evening will cause far more of a bottleneck than one knocked down first thing in the morning, as temporary repairs will be more difficult, the logistics timetable will be more disrupted, and the back-up of supply vehicles should provide a rich target through the following day.

LGBs are favoured for this type of attack, delivered, for example, by F-111Fs equipped with Pave Tack designator pods. The approach would be flown fast and low to an IP, where the nav/attack system would be updated, and at a fixed distance from the target the aircraft would pop up to acquire it on radar and release the bombs using radar aiming. Immediately after release, and while the aircraft is turning away and back to low level, the WSO in the right hand seat acquires the target on Pave Tack, which has an infra-red sensor, then switches on the laser designator to track it: the bombs should then acquire the laser reflections and home on them. The process sounds very simple, but in fact it is very difficult and requires a long period of intense training. The pilot has to fly a carefully calculated manoeuvre manually in darkness, while the WSO has to operate Pave Tack while being flung around the sky, sometimes half inverted, concentrating solely on holding the designator on target.

Defence suppression is an inevitable part of any deep penetration mission. While aircraft like Tornado and many others can carry antiradiation missiles, the USAF has a specialised defence suppression aircraft, the F-4G Wild Weasel, fitted with an electronic system which can detect and classify hostile radar emis-

F-111 Pave Tack deployment

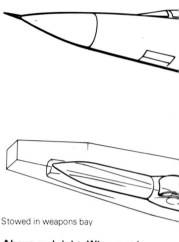

Stowed in weapons bay

Above and right: When not in use the Pave Tack pod is stowed in an F-111F's weapons bay. On the approach to the target it is lowered and rotated and pointed within the limits shown.

Below: Pave Tack combines a Flir viewing system which enables the Weapon Systems Officer to designate a target with a laser ranger/ designator for accuracy.

Pave Tack operation

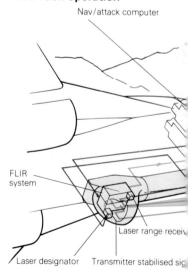

Nav/attack computer

FLIR system

Laser range receiv

Laser designator   Transmitter stabilised sig

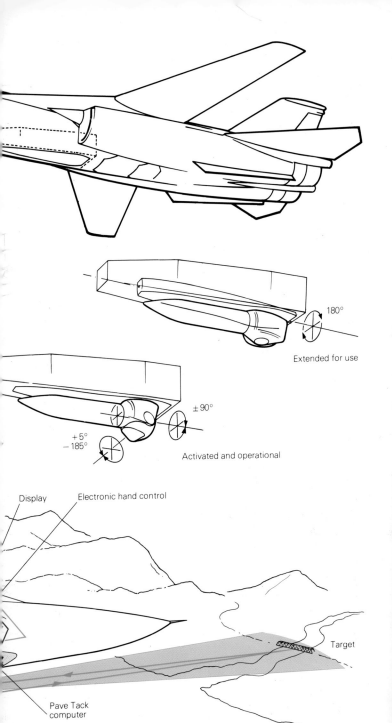

180°

Extended for use

±90°

+5°
−185°

Activated and operational

Display Electronic hand control

Target

Pave Tack
computer

sions; with a minimum of three bearings, it can pinpoint missile radars and attack them. It flies low, occasionally popping up above the radar horizon to receive emissions and take bearings. The types and locations of radars are collected and stored, and when sufficient is known about the defences in a certain area, the attack begins. Wild Weasels operate in pairs, an F-4G teamed with an F-4E, whose function is only to attack; this would be co-ordinated from different directions, using anti-radiation missiles and CBUs. Ideally, the team would consist of two F-4Gs, but they are expensive, and there are not enough of them to go round.

F-4Gs would be used to support strike forces, defence suppression not being an end in itself. Weasel effectiveness may well be improved in the future by the use of Situational Awareness Technology, or SAT, which is currently under development by LTV Aerospace. This teams three F-16s, equipped with a SAT display fed by data link, with a single F-4G. The F-4G thus becomes a hunter with a killer F-16 on his wing, plus a pair of F-16 killers in attendance. The detection data gathered by the F-4G is passed to the F-16s, which launch co-ordinated attacks on the targets.

Finally, there is the anti-ship mission. This is accomplished mainly by stealth, with missile-carrying aircraft flying out to the search area at low level before climbing to a few thousand feet for a quick radar scan. If a target is found the coordinates are fed into the navigation system of the missile, which is then launched, flying most of the way at low level on a preprogrammed course before switching to on-board homing, usually active radar, for the final leg. It is possible for the detecting aircraft to pass the data onto a companion at a considerable distance, and still at low level, who will then launch a missile from a position undetectable by the surface ships. This is essentially a medium- to long-range form of attack, and the requirements of the aircraft carrying it out are simply an adequate radar and the ability to carry the missile a reasonable distance and launch it. Of course, if the target happened to be an American carrier task

group defended by the Hawkeye/Tomcat combination, it would also need a lot of luck.

Right: With four Kormoran, Sea Eagle or Harpoon missiles, Tornado has a range in the maritime strike role of better than 700nm from base to the weapon's stand-off range. Optimum altitude cruise out and back is combined with a high-speed dash to the release point.

Right: Harpoon is launched at a typical stand-off range of 50nm and at medium altitude. It is programmed to dive to low level for the inertially guided mid-course phase, then to sea-skimming height for the active radar-guided terminal phase.

Below: Following a similar attack profile, Kormoran hits just above the waterline.

Tornado maritime strike

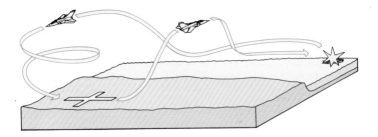

Harpoon attack

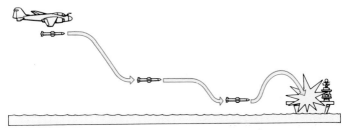

OTHER SUPER-VALUE MILITARY GUIDES IN THIS SERIES

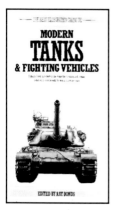

OTHER ILLUSTRATED MILITARY GUIDES AVAILABLE

Modern US Fighters and Attack Aircraft
Modern US Navy
Modern Warships
Modern US Army
Modern Elite Forces

★ Each title has 160 fact-filled pages
★ Each is colorfully illustrated with hundreds of action photographs and technical drawings
★ Each contains concisely presented data and accurate descriptions of major international weapons systems
★ Each title represents tremendous value for money